Henry Close, ThM

Ceremonies for Spiritual Healing and Growth

*Pre-publication
REVIEWS,
COMMENTARIES,
EVALUATIONS . . .*

"This is not your ordinary book of liturgy; this is a very personal, slightly offbeat, and delightfully skewed treatment of life's transitions in liturgical form. It is also grounded in good theology, supported by thoughtful therapeutic values, and informed by a lifetime of pastoral care and counseling. Still, the greatest gift of this book may lie not in the liturgies, but in the way they start you thinking about the therapeutic role of theology as it is expressed in liturgy. Henry Close reminds us through these ceremonies that the work of the pastor is to contextualize what might otherwise seem to be an individualized—and therefore isolated and alien—experience. He reminds us that we are humans, before God and one another, no matter who or where we are, and he invites us to offer that humanity to God and one another. And that is the heart of liturgy."

Paul K. Hooker, DMin, PhD
*Executive Presbyter and Stated Clerk,
Presbytery of St. Augustine,
Presbyterian Church (USA)*

"Where can we turn when the extraordinary is called for—the funeral for a prodigal son, a service for adoption or for divorce, the ceremony for a stop-smoking commitment, or for moving a loved one from home to nursing home, or for turning off a life-support system? With pastoral sensitivity for people of various faith traditions, Henry Close offers creative resources for the planning and conduction of such services as well as for weddings and funerals in more ordinary situations."

Wade Huie, PhD
*Peter Marshall Chair of Homiletics,
Emeritus, Columbia Theological Seminary*

"Close gifts the pastoral care world with a creative and original book that melds well-researched academic and professional perspectives. Pastors, therapists, church worship committees—all who nurture the communities which nurture the sojourner traveling in critical times—will want to read, mark, and inwardly digest this soul-expanding document."

Rev. A. Kempton Haynes Jr.
*Supervisor Emeritus, Association
for Clinical Pastoral Education*

More pre-publication
REVIEWS, COMMENTARIES, EVALUATIONS . . .

"In *Ceremonies for Spiritual Healing and Growth* Henry Close thoughtfully and tenderly offers long overdue ceremonies for significant life transitions and situations. His theological sensitivity and scriptural grounding interweave with his pastoral wisdom to provide powerful resources for individuals, families, and communities. A real master, Close has filled this book with messages for healing on all levels: physical, mental, emotional, and spiritual. This is a much-needed resource for pastors and therapists."

Virginia Felder, DMin
*Marriage and Family Therapist
and Presbyterian Minister,
Tucker, Georgia*

The Haworth Pastoral Press®
An Imprint of The Haworth Press, Inc.
New York • London • Oxford

Ceremonies for Spiritual Healing and Growth

Ceremonies for Spiritual Healing and Growth

Henry Close, ThM

The Haworth Pastoral Press®
An Imprint of The Haworth Press, Inc.
New York • London • Oxford

For more information on this book or to order, visit
http://www.haworthpress.com/store/product.asp?sku=5590

or call 1-800-HAWORTH (800-429-6784) in the United States and Canada
or (607) 722-5857 outside the United States and Canada

or contact orders@HaworthPress.com

Published by

The Haworth Pastoral Press®, an imprint of The Haworth Press, Inc., 10 Alice Street, Binghamton, NY 13904-1580.

PUBLISHER'S NOTE
The development, preparation, and publication of this work has been undertaken with great care. However, the Publisher, employees, editors, and agents of The Haworth Press are not responsible for any errors contained herein or for consequences that may ensue from use of materials or information contained in this work. The Haworth Press is committed to the dissemination of ideas and information according to the highest standards of intellectual freedom and the free exchange of ideas. Statements made and opinions expressed in this publication do not necessarily reflect the views of the Publisher, Directors, management, or staff of The Haworth Press, Inc., or an endorsement by them.

Identities and circumstances of individuals discussed in this book have been changed to protect confidentiality.

The Haworth Press, Inc., 10 Alice Street, Binghamton, NY 13904-1580.

Cover design by Jennifer M. Gaska.

Library of Congress Cataloging-in-Publication Data

Close, Henry T., Th. M.
 Ceremonies for spiritual healing and growth / Henry Close.
  p. cm.
 Includes bibliographical references and index.
 ISBN-13: 978-0-7890-2904-1 (hc. : alk. paper)
 ISBN-10: 0-7890-2904-9 (hc. : alk. paper)
 ISBN-13: 978-0-7890-2905-8 (pbk. : alk. paper)
 ISBN-10: 0-7890-2905-7 (pbk. : alk. paper)
 1. Rites and ceremonies. 2. Life change events—Religious aspects—Christianity. 3. Spiritual healing. 4. Spiritual formation. I. Title.

BV178.C56 2006
265—dc22

2005031516

This book is dedicated
with deep appreciation
to my wife,

Hope,

who has helped me understand the ceremonial qualities
possible in a marriage.

ABOUT THE AUTHOR

Henry Close, ThM, is a respected leader and innovator in pastoral counseling. A member until retirement of the American Association of Pastoral Counselors (Diplomate) and the American Association for Marriage and Family Therapy, he has taught in Columbia Seminary's doctoral program and given many seminars throughout the United States and also abroad. He has written two books and over 50 professional articles. *Metaphor in Psychotherapy* was a 1999 selection of the Behavioral Science Book Service and also the Psychotherapy Book Club. *Becoming a Forgiving Person* was published by The Haworth Press, Inc., in 2004. His abiding interest is in what he calls "the languages of the heart," which includes both metaphor and ceremony. These are the "languages" that effectively lead to change and growth.

CONTENTS

Acknowledgments

In my work as a pastoral counselor/marriage and family therapist, I have had several occasions to create formal religious ceremonies to address a client's needs. These ceremonies seem to have helped people through some difficult times.

Most of these ceremonies were created for specific persons dealing with specific issues. Others, such as the wedding service, are more generic and have been used many times. Some are hypothetical, as are some of the people I have described, and have not actually been used. My purpose here is to present the best I have to offer, not to give a newspaper account of what actually happened.

Thanks to those of you for whom these ceremonies were written. I have made every effort to protect your identities. Many times I think even you would not recognize yourselves. Half the people referred to as female were in reality male, and vice versa.

Thanks to the many people who have influenced me over the years. Special thanks to Burrell Dinkins, Jenny Felder, and Wade Huie. Your friendship, encouragement, and support have meant a lot to me.

Thanks also to the following publications for permission to use material originally published in their pages: Impact Publishers; *The Journal of Pastoral Care and Counseling; The American Journal of Family Therapy; Pilgrimage;* and *VOICES: The Art and Science of Psychotherapy.* Appropriate credit has been given in each case.

Author's Note

On a few occasions, I have used the masculine pronoun for God. Some of those times have involved the benediction ("The Lord bless you and keep you . . ."). I love this benediction, but I have never found a way to say it in gender-neutral terms without it being grammatically abominable and sounding terribly awkward. If you have an answer to this dilemma, please write me.

At other times, I assumed that the people for whom the ceremonies were written were most familiar with masculine pronouns for God. The purpose of the ceremony is to tap into the deepest resources of someone's faith. These resources usually stem from childhood and are encoded in the memory in the language of that period of a person's life. To use a different language—however correct—might well be a distraction. In the ceremony on smoking, I simply used the language of AA.

My purpose in writing this book is to offer some material that you might be able to use. A broader purpose is to stimulate your interest and imagination in creating your own ceremonies.

doi:10.1300/5590_b

Introduction

An Adoption Ceremony

A family therapist once saw a family with four children: Adam, who was twelve; Betsy, who was eleven; Charlie, who was eight; and Alan, who was seven. Charlie had been adopted a year or so earlier. His birth mother, a serious drug abuser, had finally given up trying to raise him and had entrusted him to an elderly aunt. When the aunt could no longer care for him, she asked a neighbor family with whom he was close to adopt him, which they did. To everyone's horror, the birth mother died of a drug overdose the very day of the adoption.

Adam seemed to welcome Charlie into the family as an ally: "Us brothers have to stick together!" Betsy and Alan, on the other hand, viewed Charlie as a competitor for parental attention, and had a hard time with the transition.

Charlie's concerns were typical of many adopted children: Would his new parents love him as much as their "real" children? Would he be treated fairly? Would his brothers and sister tease him about being different? Would he be abandoned by this family also?

His anxieties sometimes expressed themselves in violent temper tantrums. He said it was like he had a red-hot band of iron squeezing his head. This is what made him act so terrible. Out of these concerns, the family consulted a warm and nurturing family therapist. Magda talked a great deal with Charlie about family, abandonment, control, and the broader meanings of adoption. She finally asked Charlie if *he* would like to adopt his parents. She felt this would give him a sense of power in a situation in which he had very little control.

The ceremony in this chapter was adapted from my article "An Adoption Ceremony," *The Journal of Pastoral Care and Counseling,* Winter 1993, and is used with the publisher's permission.

doi:10.1300/5590_01

1

Charlie thought that this was a great idea. So they planned to have a ceremony in Magda's office with the whole family present.

Knowing of my interests in ceremonies, Magda asked me to create an appropriate ceremony for her to use with the family.

THE MEANING OF ADOPTION

"Beloved family, we are here today to celebrate one of the most important occasions in all of life: the choosing of a family. In most families these choices and commitments are made little by little, without anybody really being aware of them. But in a very real sense, all children need to be adopted by their parents, and all parents need to be adopted by their children. They need to affirm, 'We love you because we *choose* to, not just because you are here. It is by deliberate decision that we take you into our hearts and give our hearts to you.' This is as much a need for the children as for the parents, for there is a deep mutuality that emerges in the process of becoming a family.

"True love is never competitive. It is impossible to love one person less just because you love another person also, for love is not a thing that can be divided up. Love is an energy, a spirit, a strength: the more it is used the stronger and more full of life it becomes. The more you love one person, the more able you are to love others. Biological ties of course are very real and very important, but spiritual ties are even more real and more important. [The old saying, "blood is thicker than water," needs to be amended by adding, "but milk is thicker than blood!"] Ultimately, love is more real than physical kinship, for without the heart there is no life at all. One's real parents are those who *love* them; one's real children are those who love them and who are loved by them."

Prayer

"Loving God, You have not only breathed into each of us the breath of life, You have taken us into Your own heart as well. You have adopted us into Your own family and blessed us with Your love. So now in this sacred moment of affirmation, may we know that You are present, and that You bless this family in a special way as they now acknowledge their commitment to each other. Amen."

ACCEPTANCE OF RESPONSIBILITY

"Do you, Charlie, take Holly and Mark to be your true and loving parents, and do you commit yourself to being their true and loving son, to share with them your joys and your sorrows, to forgive them for their mistakes, to appreciate them for their love, to learn from them, and enjoy them even beyond the years of your growing up?

"And do you take Adam, Betsy, and Alan to be your true and loving brothers and sister, and do you commit yourself to being their brother, to know them and enjoy them, to forgive them for their mistakes, to make them your friend, and for you to be their friend, even beyond the years of your growing up?

"And do you, Holly and Mark, take Charlie to be your own true and loving son, and do you commit yourselves to being his true and loving parents, to take him into your hearts, to make him feel special, to forgive him for his mistakes, to love and enjoy him even beyond the years of his growing up?

"And do you now reaffirm your love and commitment to your other children, Adam and Betsy and Alan, and do you commit yourselves anew . . .?

"And do you, Adam and Betsy and Alan, take Charlie to be your true and loving brother . . .?

"And do you, Adam and Betsy and Alan, reaffirm Holly and Mark as your true and loving parents . . .?"

AN ALLEGORY ON BEING A FAMILY

"In the middle of a large forest there was a small clearing, with just two beautiful trees in it. As these trees grew, they shared many things. They shared the wind that blew in their branches. They shared the birds that sat in their midst and filled the air with singing. They shared the sun that shone on their leaves. They shared the gentle rain that fell around them to nourish them. They shared the ground on which they stood.

"As the roots from these two trees reached farther and farther out into the world, they finally touched each other and became entwined in each other. The trees felt very close to each other and knew they belonged together. Gradually they realized they loved each other. After awhile, another tree began to grow between the two large trees, and then another one, and then another. They had become a family.

"One day there was a terrible fire in another part of the forest. Many of the trees were burned—some of them were burned very painfully, and a few of them were completely destroyed.

"After the fire, one of the foresters noticed a beautiful little tree that had survived the fire. Some of its leaves had been singed, but it was basically a very strong and healthy tree. But one of the trees that had been its parent had been burned very badly, and the other had been burned to the ground, so that the beautiful little tree was left all alone.

"The forester realized that it was not good for this little tree to grow up in this barren place, so he very carefully took his shovel and dug all around the little tree. Finally he could lift it out of the ground with lots of good soft earth clinging to its roots. He put it in a large basket and started looking for a good place to transplant it.

"As he walked through the forest, he came within sight of the other tree family. Immediately these two tall and beautiful trees understood. They looked at the ground beneath them. They looked at each other. They looked at their own three offspring. They noticed a nice vacant place between them that would be ideal for transplanting another tree. They wanted this beautiful little tree transplanted in their midst, to become part of their family. So they began to move their branches and rustle their leaves to get the forester's attention.

"When he looked in their direction, they both pointed with their branches to the ground between them. As the forester walked over to them, he knew in his heart that this was the place to transplant the little tree.

"Very carefully he began to dig a nice big hole in which to plant the beautiful little tree. But some of the roots from the big trees had grown over into this area, and some of the roots of the little trees had grown over there too. So when the forester dug in with his shovel, he cut some of these other roots—and that hurt a little bit. One of the little trees even cried. But they knew deep in their hearts that anything worthwhile sometimes hurts a little, and the hurt made the beautiful little tree even more important to them.

"Finally the forester was finished. He placed the little tree in the hole, patted down the soft earth around him, poured on lots of water, and told the little tree he hoped he would be very happy there.

"At first the little tree was somewhat scared. He didn't understand about the fire. He didn't understand about his parent trees being hurt so badly. He didn't understand the forester digging up the ground around him and cutting some of his roots too. He didn't understand being carried through the forest and being transplanted in the midst of another family. No, there were lots of things this little tree did not understand.

"Very gradually the other trees began to reach out to him. They didn't want to do too much too quickly, for the little tree was very shy at first. But day after day they would point out a lovely flower that had just bloomed and was filling the world with fragrance, or they would be very quiet so that he could hear a bird singing in the distance. On a very hot day, they would shield him with their leaves and branches to protect him from the sun, and during a terrible storm they hovered around him to shield him from the harshness of the wind.

"When he asked why they were treating him so lovingly, they simply said, 'You're one of us now. You are part of our family.'

"As the trees grew taller and stronger and healthier, their roots all grew together and their branches became intertwined. Sometimes they would be playing together, sometimes teasing, sometimes supporting each other, sometimes arguing. But the more they grew, the more they realized, 'We belong together. We are a family.'"

EXCHANGE OF GIFTS

(It would be appropriate for each sibling to give a gift to the adopted child and perhaps each other as well—something that was precious to the person at one time, but that he or she is now ready to give up. The adopted child should also give a similar gift to each sibling. Maybe the gift is just a note on a card, offering to do something special for the other person. The parents should give a gift of some kind to each child. The children should not give anything to the parents. This is especially important for the adopted child, who needs to know that nothing is required of him or her by the parents.)

"In the exchanging of gifts, we recognize that we give and we receive from one another, that to have another person in our lives will sometimes cost us something and will sometimes enrich us."

DECLARATION

Following the Lord's prayer, the leader would say, "You have chosen in a very special way to be a family and to affirm that on this special day. Along with you, I am happy to acknowledge that and to encourage you to be the best and the happiest family that you can possibly be."

❧

Magda proposed the adoption ceremony to the parents after the session in which she raised it with Charlie. When they told the family, Adam and Alan seemed a bit indifferent, but Betsy was angry. The ceremony made the adoption real—something she had been denying. She was particularly irate at the thought that Charlie had a choice of his family, whereas she had none.

Betsy's anger seemed to trigger a few days of general upset in the family, so much so that the father and Charlie made a special appointment to see Magda. Father talked about problems he had had with his father, which seemed to be brought to the surface at this time.

Picking out gifts to give Charlie was particularly hard for Adam, Betsy, and Alan. Three times the parents called to postpone the ceremony.

Finally they met together in Magda's office with everyone dressed well. Betsy seemed petulant and defiant; Charlie was profoundly attentive. When in the ceremony they were asked to acknowledge their acceptance of each other, instead of saying the expected "I do," Charlie said, "Yes ma'am," spoken softly and intently, with utter seriousness. Even Betsy seemed to respond more positively when asked for her commitment to her new brother, especially at the thought that she could gain a sense of importance by having someone to teach and protect.

At the exchange of gifts (which were nicely wrapped), Adam gave Betsy a poster he had been given by their grandfather, and which Betsy had always envied; he gave Charlie an autographed baseball he had prized for years; he gave Alan a baseball cap that had been given to him by their uncle.

Betsy gave Adam a malachite egg that Grandfather had sent her from Africa; she gave Charlie a stuffed bear that she had slept with for years—up to the previous night; she gave Alan her favorite book of nursery stories!

Charlie gave Adam, Betsy, and Alan three framed pictures that had been taken of him and them four years earlier when he had been visiting their family—pictures he had kept on his dresser all these years. Magda took this to mean that these pictures had symbolized hope; now that Charlie was in this new world, he no longer needed the symbol.

Father, whose hobby was wood turning, gave each child a goblet carved from a different rare wood. Before the ceremony, he had given each child a letter.

Mother had also written a letter to each child. She moved over and sat next to each child in turn to read the letter to him or her—thus affirming the uniqueness and individuality of each child. In each letter she told of her love for them and asked their forgiveness for her mistakes as a parent. All members of the family were openly weeping during this time. Magda then asked the father to close with prayer, which he did with deep feeling.

They then had refreshments. While they were informally snacking, Charlie asked Magda if she was very rich. Magda said there were many kinds of richness. You can have a rich cake or an expensive car. You can also be rich in friends, and a family can be very rich in love.

This ceremony was a powerful experience for this family, addressing the family as a unit and as individuals, bringing a sense of reality to the adoption and renewing their sense of love and commitment to one another.

A couple of weeks afterward, Charlie was talking with his mother and referred to the ceremony. He said that before he heard the story, he hadn't understood what had happened to him, but now he did. And the band of red-hot iron around his head was gone.

༺༻

Ceremonial rituals like this one seem to be universal in human experience. They address something very deep and basic in the human psyche. In the life cycle, there are many changes, transitions, in which a person moves from one role in the community to another, from one identity to another. These transitions call for new ways of relating to the world, new responsibilities, new ways of thinking of oneself. This inevitably creates anxiety.

Ceremonies address the difficulties of change. Using what I call the languages of the heart to address issues of the heart, a ceremony bypasses the sterility of logic and analysis and evokes a power to heal that straightforward rational communication cannot touch (see my book *Metaphor in Psychotherapy* for a discussion of the differences between these two "languages").

All transitions involve separation and loss. There is a separation from that which is familiar and a commitment to that which is unknown. The movement is usually from some state of dependence to a greater responsibility. Often, one's place in the community changes. A ceremony acknowledges the loss and affirms one's commitment to a new future and a new place in one's community.

A ceremony has the quality of set-apartness from the ordinary activities of life, or investing these activities with a quality of specialness. It affirms that there are other levels of reality in addition to the mundane. It invites us into these other levels of living, not to negate the other realities of life, but to provide another perspective on them.

The military has always understood the power of ritual and ceremony and used it to numb people to the difficulties of military service. Dictators and other riff-raff (as Paul Watzlawick so deliciously puts it) also understand the power of ritual and its ability to enable people to endure hardship. The Nazis, for instance, were especially attentive to the use of ritual and ceremony.

In Hebrew history, the people were provided with a goat onto which they could project their sins. They would lay their hands on the goat while the priest pronounced the ritual words. The goat was then driven into the wilderness, thus symbolically allowing the people to distance themselves from their sins. This is the origin of the word "scapegoat."

A ceremony always involves one's community in some way. The leader is often a representative of one's spiritual tradition. Other members of the community are often present. And if the ceremony is done in private, others are at least present in the participant's imagination. Ceremonies also involve God, whose presence is acknowledged and whose blessing is assured.

Some transitions are extremely painful, such as a funeral. Others celebrate happy transitions in life, such as a wedding. Some of these ceremonies presented here were designed for use in public. Others are meant to be used in the privacy of a therapist's or pastor's office.

PART I:
CEREMONIES FOR HEALING

Chapter 1

Divorce

Divorce is an increasingly common reality in our time. It is an extremely painful transition, complicated by the complex feelings of loss, confusion, anger, guilt, helplessness, despair, and more. The spirit, the mood of the ceremony that is offered here is similar to that of a funeral. A marriage has died, and this death needs to be recognized and grieved. The people involved need the close support of their friends, their church, their God, so that they may get on with the task of grieving and building a new life.

It should also be a time of commitment, a commitment to treat each other with kindness and respect, and not to involve their children in disagreements.

A friend who read this service said that if people could cooperate enough to participate in a service like this, they would not need to divorce. Perhaps he is right. It would take an exceptional couple to do this.

I have never actually used this service. But if I did, I would ask that only family and perhaps a very few special friends attend—friends who were supportive rather than critical. It may be especially important for the children to be there. They need to hear their parents commit to treating each other with respect and kindness, and to hear their commitment not to involve the children in their disputes.

In the hypothetical ceremony presented here, Paul and Susan are divorcing after twelve years of marriage. Their two children, Thomas and Lucy, are ten and eight, respectively.

The ceremony in this chapter was adapted from my article "A Service of Divorce," *Pilgrimage,* Spring 1977, and is used with the publisher's permission.

doi:10.1300/5590_02

PRINCIPLES OF DIVORCE

"We are here today with sadness, to bear witness to the painful side of our human existence, to the part of life that is associated with death. We bear witness humbly today to the death of a marriage, and to the death of the dreams, the hopes, the expectations that brought this relationship into being. Somehow these aspirations were not fulfilled. In spite of noble purposes, of good intentions, of sincere effort, this marriage has died, and the process of grieving has begun.

"We here today stand with you in your grieving, to affirm our ties with you, our support for you in this anxious time of transition and rebuilding, and to affirm very clearly your place in the community of God's people. Marriage is a difficult venture, and there can never be guarantees of its success. It is to your credit that you tried.

"You have been as two trees that were transplanted so close together that their limbs and branches became intertwined. As they grew, the trees together formed one canopy. They influenced each other—permanently. When the time came that the trees were separated, torn apart, there were painful wounds where the trunks had grown together. Roots were torn and branches were broken.

"As both trees are transplanted again, they face the struggle of putting down new roots to sustain them and growing new branches with which to reach out to their world."

A CHARGE TO THE COUPLE

"As you, Paul and Susan, have reluctantly committed yourselves to this separating and transplanting, you will experience a confusing array of feelings of relief and regret, of hope and fear, of frustration, and perhaps most of all, of uncertainty. But the step has been taken, and it is important now to follow this new course wisely and to find fulfillment in a new way of life.

"As you commit yourselves to the process of creatively un-marrying, I offer to you several challenges:

"I invite you to forgive each other. At this point, you will have many resentments about what your spouse was and was not, or has done and not done. Perhaps you have even told yourself that if only he or she had been different, everything would have worked out beautifully. But you cannot resent without clinging to the past, so it is important to forgive.

"I invite you to forgive yourselves. Each of you will experience guilt for what you have been and not been, for what you have done and not done, for time and energy wasted in futile activity and inactivity. But this is now behind you, and you can forgive yourselves.

"I invite you to grieve. There is much that has died and is still dying, and you will both experience a deep sense of loss. What you wanted to be, and what you wanted each other to be and the relationship to be, are all dreams that were unfulfilled, that have died. Your task now is to face these deaths, to finish the work of grieving, and to go on to what lies ahead.

"I invite you to learn. What you expected from yourselves and from each other and from marriage you did not find. Perhaps much of what you expected is not available anywhere. The ways you presented yourselves or asked for each other were not adequately effective. It is important to learn anew what you can realistically expect of life, and how to achieve it.

"I invite you to find yourselves again. Your identities have been closely intertwined with each other, and you have each given up some sense of yourself as individuals. To find yourselves again you must separate from each other without the guilt and bitterness that clings to the past, and without the naive optimism that clings to an illusion.

"I urge you treat each other with respect and kindness. Keep a soft heart toward each other. Remember that you once loved each other, and nothing can take that away from you.

"I invite you to love again. There have undoubtedly been times when you have each felt very unloving and unlovable, and perhaps have despaired of ever again risking intimacy and love. But as human beings there is a hunger within you to reach out to other people, to touch and to be touched. And I charge you this day to awaken and nourish this hunger to love and to be loved."

Prayer

"Loving God, You alone know the full implications of decisions painfully born in the crucible of disappointment. Bless now these Your people as they move through this time of parting and rebuilding. Guide them in the pathways of courage and hope and renewal. Where there has been guilt, may there be acceptance; where there has been bitterness, may there be forgiveness; where there has been a deadness of spirit, may there be life and movement and growth, in the name of Christ, Amen."

AN ACCEPTANCE OF SEPARATENESS

At this point, Paul and then Susan would read these vows to each other and to the children.

"With great sadness, Susan/Paul, I acknowledge that our marriage has ended, and I solemnly and respectfully divorce you, severing the marital ties that have united us. I apologize to you for the things I did that were destructive to our relationship.

"I also apologize to you, Thomas and Lucy, for the distress this is causing you. None of this was in any way your fault. I promise to work with your mother/father to provide you with a happy and secure home. I promise never to say negative things about your mother/father in your presence, or to ask you to take sides. We are both still your parents, and we both love you, and that will never change."

Prayer

"Eternal God, You are the God of life, who created life in the beginning, and who even now brings life out of death. We pray for new life for these Your people. Bless them, that out of this separation may come wisdom. Bring to them a new sense of Your presence, Your forgiveness, Your guidance. May they know anew that You are their God; they are Your people. Our Father, who art in heaven . . ."

ACKNOWLEDGMENT OF DIVORCE

"As a minister of Christ, I now acknowledge that this marriage has ended. Paul and Susan are no longer husband and wife. Let us therefore humbly respect the breaking of these ties."

BENEDICTION

"Now may the Lord bless you and keep you; the Lord make His face to shine upon you, and be gracious unto you; the Lord lift up the light of His countenance upon you, and give you peace; now and forevermore. Amen."

❧

I wrote this ceremony many years ago while working with a young couple on the edge of divorce. When I read it to them, the wife said with much sadness, "I really don't want that [a divorce]." Thirty years later they were still married. I think that using the language of ceremony to discuss divorce brought home its reality in a way that ordinary language could not and helped them understand that divorce would not solve all their problems.

The feedback about this ceremony has been strongly positive. A minister friend gave it to one of his parishioners who was profoundly depressed after the breakup of her marriage. She told him that this ceremony probably saved her life. This speaks of the power of the language of ceremony. I am sure other people must have told her all the things that are in the ceremony, but the language of ceremony addresses a different level of the psyche than does the language of logic and factual reality.

Perhaps the most interesting use of this service was by a friend who was pastor of a very difficult small church. Within a year both he and the board realized that this was not a good "marriage," and he resigned. On the final Sunday, he used this ceremony as the basis for a sermon about loss and transition. Several people commented very favorably on the sermon, and two people asked for copies of the ceremony.

Chapter 2

A Funeral Service for an Aborted Baby

Several years ago, I had two clients, each of whom had had an abortion some five years earlier. Each was now married with a two-year-old child of her own and felt that her unresolved feelings from the abortion were interfering with her ability to be a good mother to the child she now had.

No matter what a pastor's feelings about abortion may be, he or she would most certainly want to minister compassionately to a woman in circumstances like this.

Melissa, a minister's daughter, had been raised in a home that was strict almost to the point of being abusive. As a child, she had been stubbornly rebellious toward her father, who made her feel guilty for her insubordination. As an adult, her approach to life was quite phobic. She was timid and nonassertive around other people, and generally unsure of herself and her worth.

When she went away to college, she became involved with a young man of whom the parents did not approve. This further alienated her from them and added to her already low self-esteem. Eventually she became pregnant. Marriage was not realistic for them for many reasons, so with a great sense of guilt and shame she had an abortion. This was followed by a generalized depression and phobia about life.

During her senior year, she and the young man were married and had a planned baby whom they both adored. However, Melissa's unresolved guilt about the abortion was now interfering with her ability to be a good mother.

I thought that a structured ceremony might be very helpful for Melissa. After deciding in my own mind how I would handle it, I offered

This chapter is adapted from my article "A Funeral Service for an Aborted Baby," *VOICES: The Art and Science of Psychotherapy,* Spring 1988, and is used with the publisher's permission.

doi:10.1300/5590_03

to conduct a funeral service with her for the aborted baby. I explained that human beings need some kind of transition such as a religious ceremony to help them through difficult and painful events in their lives. The terrible pressures that drive women to an abortion are seldom addressed. Some friends/family will condemn her. Others may think that what is needed is for them to exonerate her, without taking seriously her distress.

There is no funeral service for the child, who is after all innocent. (A colleague said that the word "child" is too strong a word. It is a fetus that is aborted, and the word "child" might add to the woman's guilt and distress. After much thought, I decided to retain the word "child." Women who abort a "fetus" would not have the same intense reactions as women for whom it is not a fetus, but a child. It is this identification that makes the abortion so difficult, and it is for these women that this ceremony was created.) There is no way to say goodbye to the child that might have been, no way to express the ambiguities and regrets that exist.

I explained that when an abortion is performed, the fetus is cremated. She does not have access to the ashes, so a literal burial is impossible. But she does have in her mind and heart many thoughts and feelings about the child that might have been. She has many feelings of her own about the action she took; she has things she would like to be able to say to the child who still lives in her imagination or memory.

One way to do this is in the form of a letter addressed to the child. I encourage her to give a name to the baby—a name that will not be used again with a child of hers. She can say whatever she wishes in the letter: describe what she thinks the child would have been like at this point in time; express her regrets for the abortion; explain her reasons for this choice.

I told her to take as long as she wished to compose the letter (or statement). If she had trouble expressing herself, I would be glad to offer a tentative outline of things that might be covered. When it felt appropriate to her to have the funeral, she could bring the letter to a session. She might also bring any items that symbolized the baby's life.

I asked if she would like to have anyone else with her for the funeral, such as her husband. She (and the other woman also) chose to come alone.

After a brief opening prayer, we lit a candle, and I asked the woman to read the letter aloud. These were beautiful tender letters. One brought tears to my eyes. It started, "Dear Rachel, I see you standing before me as a beautiful five-year-old girl . . ."

I deeply regret that there was no way to save a copy of this letter, but I could think of no way to do that without interfering with the sense of ending that was the primary objective of the service.

I then folded the letter and placed it in a large bowl, with an invitation to pray. Both women were traditional Christians, so the prayer was a traditional Christian prayer, using language that would be familiar and redemptive in their experience. With a different client, I would have used a different prayer. With a Jewish client, for instance, I would have consulted a rabbi and asked him or her to help me compose an appropriate prayer.

"Loving God, You are the Lord and Savior of all creatures, and You alone know fully the pressures under which we live and under which we have to make decisions—often terribly difficult decisions. You are the Lord and Maker of all life, and we all exist in Your consciousness, and in Your thoughts, and in Your caring.

"And Rachel exists in Your consciousness too, for You take into Yourself all that was and is and shall be, with caring and forgiveness and healing. Rachel's memory is expressed here, in this letter, and in the feelings that accompany it. As this letter is transformed into smoke and ashes, the spirit of this child is released to be taken up into the safety of Your caring.

"Receive now anew the spirit of this child, the prayers of her parents, and affirm for them the finishing of what is past and the reality of new beginnings from this moment, in the name of the Father, the Son, and the Holy Spirit, Amen."

At this point, I asked Melissa to burn the letter. I sat quietly with her, making occasional comments to encourage her to stay with her thoughts and feelings, and to regard those as her prayer at that moment. When the letter had burned completely, I carried the bowl with the ashes outside for burial. (The other woman carried the ashes with her in an envelope to sprinkle in a river.) After Melissa had sprinkled the ashes around the base of a rose bush, I closed with a brief prayer.

If she had brought an item that symbolized the baby's life, I would have encouraged her to bury this also.

"Now O Lord, we have committed to Your care the spirit of this child. And we commit ourselves anew to ever deeper understandings of Your forgiveness and Your caring, in the name of the Father, the Son, and the Holy Spirit, Amen."

Melissa was intensely involved in this ceremony and said it was very helpful to her. Some time later she told me that she seemed able to love the child she now had in a way that she had not been able to do earlier. Before the funeral service it was as though if she loved the child she now had, she was being disloyal to the child she had killed.

Although this ceremony was a powerful and helpful event for these women, it did not solve all their problems. We continued to work together for several months and regarded this as one important step in a long journey.

There are at least two important contraindications for the use of a ceremony like this. The first is personal. To participate with someone in a ceremony such as this is a very intimate experience, and I would not want to do this with someone whom I did not respect and feel close to.

Nor would I want to use such a ceremony with someone who would look on it as a miracle that would resolve all her difficulties. When the ceremony did not have the desired result, the woman may be left with a sense of hopelessness, thinking that nothing can really get through to her and help her.

Chapter 3

Support for a Rape Survivor

A rather shy and retiring young woman had been in a Sunday school class for several months. One Sunday Norma seemed particularly withdrawn. When asked if something was troubling her, she said with great shame that she had been raped on the steps of the church the previous Sunday night.

The class surrounded her with their support and affirmation, which seemed to make a real difference for her. They wondered what more they could do to help her.

The teacher had attended a seminar of mine and asked for my suggestions. I proposed the following ceremony. Unfortunately, I moved soon thereafter and lost touch with the teacher. I do not know if he used it or how effective it was. For purposes of clarity, I am reporting it here as though it had actually been used.

The following Sunday evening, at about the same time as the rape, the entire class met on the steps where Norma had been violated. Replicating the time and place of the assault would help make her feelings about it more accessible to her. The class formed a protective circle around Norma, interlocking their arms firmly. The leader then prayed:

"We are here tonight, O God, in anger, in outrage and hatred for what has happened to Your child, Norma. We call on You to hear our prayer of indignation, for You also hate it when one of Yours has been abused. The sacredness of this place has been violated; the sacredness of Norma's own body has been cruelly violated.

Some of the material in this chapter (the story about the painting) is from my book *Metaphor in Psychotherapy,* Chapter 8, and is used with the publisher's permission.

doi:10.1300/5590_04

"We are here today to say, 'This ought not to have been!' We stand together with her, to offer our anger and our protection, our support and our caring. And You are here too, bringing cleansing and healing and courage. May she always know that no matter what, You stand with her and love her. In the name of Christ. Amen.

"It is hard to talk about the experience of being raped, and how one recovers from that. Words are so inadequate. But sometimes a story can express things that cannot be expressed otherwise. One woman found a metaphor to be helpful.

"There was once a young woman who had been given a beautiful painting of an adolescent girl, bright-eyed and eager as she faced her life and her thrilling future. But one night, someone cruelly defaced this picture. He painted an evil horrible man in the background, with a gnarled ugly hand across the girl's face, obscuring her beauty and her pleasure in living.

"The young woman did not know what to do with the painting now. She was frightened to let anyone see it. She thought of throwing it away, and actually took it out to the trash pile three or four times before deciding to keep it.

"Finally she decided to take painting lessons. She began to learn about colors and pigments, brushes and strokes, shadows and perspective.

"When she felt she had learned enough, she studied the painting very carefully. Her first reaction was disgust, and then a kind of fright. It would be easy to feel overwhelmed by the task that lay before her.

"But she persevered. She painted over the evil person and his ugly hand.

"But to her dismay, the dark pigments of this evil man started seeping through the new paint. Try as she might, she could not cover up that malignant influence.

"She was discouraged for a while, but finally tried something else. Very carefully she took a razor blade to scrape away the pigment that defined the ugliness. At first she scraped very tentatively, removing only the surface of the ugliness. But as time progressed, she scraped more confidently. Sometimes she scraped so vigorously that she actually removed some of the underlying pigment that defined the young girl. She would then fill in the damaged area with new pigment.

"Finally she finished. Her skills as a painter were imperfect. The finished product did not look as beautiful as if it had not been damaged. Instead of a dreamlike innocence, there was now a rugged, hardy feel to the painting that was actually very appealing. She was proud to have it in her home.

"She hung it in her living room to enjoy it, and proudly shared its beauty and strength with the people she loved and who loved her."

The leader then passed out copies of a litany and led the class through it.

LEADER: Eternal God, You have promised to walk with us through the valleys of the shadow of death.

PEOPLE: Lord, hear the prayers of our neediness.

LEADER: You have promised to lift up those who have fallen, and to comfort the afflicted.

PEOPLE: Lord, hear the prayers of our pain.

LEADER: You have promised to avenge those who have been abused.

PEOPLE: Lord, hear the prayers of our wrath.

LEADER: You have promised healing to those who have been injured. You have promised strength and courage to face the tomorrows of our lives.

PEOPLE: Lord, hear our prayers.

At this time, each member of the class walked over to Norma and asked her, "Would you be comfortable with my holding your hands for a moment?"

The purpose for this question was to give her a sense of freedom and control relative to her own body.

She assented each time. The person then took her hands, looked her in the eyes and said, "Norma, I promise you that in every way I can, I will protect you."

If the person speaking had ever been raped or otherwise humiliated, she might have told Norma about that, and maybe even asked for her protection as she offered her own. That did not happen in this situation.

It would be important for the leader to discuss this aspect of the service with the class beforehand, and to tell them *not* to relate some minor offense. That would trivialize Norma's suffering.

There were many hugs and tears as people spoke to Norma.

Following this, the leader dismissed the group with a benediction: "Now may the Lord bless you and keep you; the Lord grant you peace and courage, the Lord illumine the inner assurance that you are valued and loved. Amen."

Chapter 4

The Commitment to Stop Smoking

One of the most difficult decisions for a person to make is the commitment to stop smoking—or as I prefer to say it, to achieve freedom from one's addiction. It is always better to state things positively rather than negatively. Giving up something feels like a deprivation; achieving freedom is an accomplishment.

One understanding of addictions, such as alcoholism (see Bateson, 1972), is that the addict becomes locked in a terribly competitive struggle with the bottle. It becomes a kind of game, which must be played over and over again.

What is needed is for the addict to step out of this competitive stance toward life and adopt a submissive stance. Even a game of tennis or checkers might jeopardize an alcoholic's recovery.

The genius of Alcoholics Anonymous (AA) is its emphasis on a subordinate approach to life. One surrenders to God and to the program, confesses the harm he or she has done, and adopts a stance of total honesty. These principles are relevant in recovery from other addictions as well.

A ceremony can be a very powerful embodiment of the principles of surrender and of commitment to a new approach to life.

The ceremony that is presented here is for people who have had difficulty transcending their addiction to tobacco. It might be adapted to address other addictions as well. An appropriate time and place are chosen. Ideally, the ceremony is held out of doors, in a place where things can be buried in the ground. One's yard is probably not a good place, since you want to put as much distance as possible between yourself and cigarettes. Bring to the ceremony a shovel and a large rock.

The officiant should be someone who represents the community, such as a minister, therapist, or doctor. Do not have a member of the

doi:10.1300/5590_05

family lead the ceremony—especially someone who has pressured the person to stop smoking. There are too many power struggles in a family.

Prior to the ceremony, ask the person involved to write four thoughtful statements:

1. A vision of his or her future as it might have been had this addiction continued. Phrasing it this way implies that the addiction has already been conquered. To say "*if* the addiction continues" introduces an element of doubt. That is not what the addict needs to hear.
2. A vision of how life will be different now that the addiction has been left behind.
3. A list of the rationalizations he or she has used in the past to justify smoking.
4. A letter addressed to his or her family and friends.

To require these statements gives importance to the event. It also reinforces the new subordinate stance toward life that can transcend the competitiveness of an addiction. The officiant should call the person a few days before the ceremony is to take place. If the statements have not been written, the ceremony should be postponed. This may seem rather high-handed, but the addict needs all the help he or she can get to step out of a competitive stance toward life and into a subordinate stance.

The person should keep the first two statements in a special place and refer to them occasionally. Bring the third statement to the ceremony. The fourth statement, the letter, will be read during the ceremony.

In this letter, the person first says he realizes how destructive his smoking has been to himself and his family. He then acknowledges he is powerless over the addiction to cigarettes, and turns his life over to God. He then apologizes to the people who have suffered from his addiction to smoking—especially to his family.

Plan to have a dozen or so guests—friends and family. When people first arrive, have a few snacks. Then go together to the place for the ceremony. Following the ceremony, have a party.

The ceremony begins when all the guests have arrived. Go to the selected place, and have the guests totally encircle the person to whom the ceremony is addressed. The officiant then leads the ceremony.

Be sure to modify this ceremony to suit the particular situation and persons involved. For instance, remove the references to Christ if the person does not embrace the Christian religion.

INTRODUCTION

"Friends and family, we're here today to add our support and courage and love to Wayne as he makes a major commitment to a new life. He is saying YES to a new beginning, to health, and to life. We are saying to him, 'We care about you. We surround you with our support and our love.'

"I would like for you, Wayne, to look around you. Look each person in the eye for a moment, beginning with friends and ending with family. Take into yourself their caring and their love for you."

Pause for a few moments while he does this.

"Being held prisoner by an addiction, Wayne, feeling helpless, is a very painful thing, as you well know. At the beginning, cigarettes were friends. They helped you to be accepted by your peer group. They helped you feel adult and masculine. As time went by, they helped soften the anxieties and tensions of the day. They were your friends.

"But many times in life, a friend becomes an enemy. That which once enriched your life is now destroying it, and it is time to say good-bye. Other priorities have become more important. But like any friends that have had to be rejected, you will sometimes miss them. Just remember that anxiety is a small price to pay for your future.

"As you say good-bye to the addiction, you are saying hello in a new way to your own future and to those who love you and whom you love.

"You have tried a number of things in the past to leave this addiction behind. Don't regard those efforts as failures. They each contributed important learnings, ingredients, which you can now draw together to help you meet the challenges of a new life.

"Many people, when they stumble, use that as an excuse to resume smoking. You don't need to do that. Forgive yourself and pick up where you left off. Don't begin anew, but begin where you left off."

Prayer

"Let us pray. Loving God, You are the God of all things. In the midst of death, You speak of life. In the midst of defeat and despair,

You speak of confidence and hope. In the midst of shame, You speak of acceptance and love. Bless now Your servant, that he may feel Your presence with him, surrounding him with Your love and grace. In the name of Christ, Amen."

COMMITMENT

"Wayne, you know the questions I am going to ask you. If you are not yet ready to answer them in the affirmative, please say so. We will all adjourn to your house for refreshments and be ready to stand with you again on another occasion. Submitting to someone else's pressure to quit is like submitting to the pressure of an addiction. What is needed is for this decision to come from within you.

"Are you ready for me to continue?

"Do you solemnly turn your life over to God, as you understand Him, and with His help, commit yourself to leaving behind this addiction to smoking?

"Do you now forgive yourself for the things that led to this addiction?

"Do you forgive yourself for the rationalizations you have used to justify smoking?

"Do you forgive the people who have badgered you about your smoking when you were not yet ready to leave the addiction behind?

"Do you commit yourself to asking for help when you need it?

"And will you, loved ones and friends, support Wayne in this commitment by forgiving him and being his friend?

"Will you now read the letter you have written for this occasion?"

He reads the letter. The leader then continues.

"I have asked Wayne to bring some things with him today: cigarettes, ashtrays, and other objects related to smoking. I have also asked him to write out a list of the rationalizations he has used in the past. I would like for us now to participate together in digging a hole in which to bury these things, putting them away forever."

Every person removes a shovelful of dirt from the hole.

"Now, Wayne, would you place all these symbols of addiction in the ground, to distance yourself from them, to remove them from your life." (He does so.)

"You are the first one, Wayne, to throw some dirt on those things." (He does so.)

"Now I would like for everybody else to put in some dirt also. Then stomp on that place—stomp hard!" (They do so.)

"Now, Wayne, would you stand there while I pray, and will the rest of you place your hands on his shoulders?"

Prayer

"Loving God, we know that You support Wayne in this decision today. May Your peace descend on him, and fill him with serenity. Let all the facets of the addiction flow out of his body, down through his feet, and into the ground that is the eternal resting place of the compulsion to smoke.

"And will you join me in praying the Lord's Prayer: Our Father, Who art in heaven . . ."

AFFIRMATION

"Now would you all place the rock on that spot, so that everything there is out of Wayne's life once and for all." (They do so.)

BENEDICTION

"Let us pray. Now may the Lord bless you and keep you . . .
"A warm handshake or hug would now be appropriate."

In AA, there is a kind of celebration after a full year of sobriety. Something similar would be appropriate for the person who has left behind the compulsion to smoke—maybe an anniversary every year until it no longer feels necessary.

Chapter 5

A Refugee Child on a Visit Home

In a school in Atlanta, about 50 percent of the students are refugees. Anah, a third grade student from Bosnia, had always been her grandmother's favorite grandchild—very close and very dear to her. When the grandmother, who was still in Bosnia, realized she was dying, she asked Anah and her mother to return to see her one last time. Anah's teacher, Sister Patty Caraher, created a ceremony to mark the occasion.

The day of the ceremony, Patty spent a few minutes with each child to ask what he or she would like to say to Anah, and helped them write those thoughts on cards to give Anah.

Later that day, the students gathered in a room Patty had prepared for the occasion. In the middle of the room was a globe, and next to it was a photo of Anah's grandmother. Patty struck a chime to focus the kids' attention, and then spoke.

"We are here together as family to say good-bye to Anah and her mother as they travel very far away to see Anah's grandmother in Bosnia." Patty pointed to Bosnia on the globe, and then to Atlanta. "Anah's grandmother is very sick and she wants to see Anah and her mother. Grandmothers are very special people. They love us in wonderful ways and we love them."

Then Patty asked each student to say the word "grandmother" in his or her native language: Spanish, Farsi, Pashtu (from Afghanistan), Mauritanian, Vietnamese, Kurdish, and Bosnian. Then she asked the English-speaking kids to say all the words they knew for grandmother: Granny, Grandma, Nana, and so forth.

Patty struck the chime again and said, "Now close your eyes for a few minutes and think about your grandmother. Try to picture her in

---

Sister Caraher kindly gave me permission to use this material.

© 2006 by The Haworth Press, Inc. All rights reserved.
doi:10.1300/5590_06

your mind. Pretend she is here. What might you want to say to your grandmother? Maybe thank her for something? Maybe tell her why she is special to you? Maybe tell her you love her?"

She then had the kids say something about their grandmother(s), with Anah speaking last. Then some of the children read good-byes that Patty had written down for them:

"Anah, you are going on a long journey. We will think of you in Bosnia."

"We will miss you very much. We send you with our love."

"May the road ahead of you be free from harm. May you stay safe and secure."

"We are sending you to your grandmother who is waiting for you with love. Sit with her. Hold her hand. Be good to her."

"When you hug her, tell her that you bring lots of hugs from your friends at International Community School."

"Listen to her stories. Put them in your heart and treasure them all of your life."

Patty then asked other kids to read the notes they had written on their going-away cards. Anah was then given the cards, plus a suitcase for her trip. The group sang a song and adjourned to another room for refreshments.

This ceremony seemed to touch something very deep in the children's psyches. There was much crying, even after they had left the room. One refugee child told an American child, "You get to see your grandmother every day, but our grandmothers live very far away. We hardly ever get to see them."

(A service similar to this might address the death of a student's loved one, or the death of a fellow student or a teacher.)

Chapter 6

A Memorial Service
for One Killed in War

One of the most difficult challenges in all of life is dealing with a death that is senseless. Death in old age is expected. Death from a disease is understandable. Even death in an accident is a tragic extension of something we are all familiar with. But death caused by the random violence of strangers is so bewildering that there are no models in our culture for dealing with it.

There are many places in the world where just such tragedies occur, sometimes in the context of war, sometimes terrorism, sometimes without even those rationalizations.

The death of a healthy man in middle age is also a rending of the natural order. We expect to bury our parents, even our spouse in old age. No one expects to bury a man in his thirties. A young child does not expect to bury his father, nor an elderly father his son. Our sense of order in the world is shaken.

The memorial service that is offered here was created for the family and friends of a Bosnian man who was killed in a Serbian concentration camp, and then buried in a common grave. The family had been in this country for just a few months when they got word of Ahmed's death. A friend who has been active in refugee work asked me to create a memorial service for him.

In this situation, some of the family called themselves Christian and some called themselves Muslim. But having lived under Communist domination all their lives, none had had the opportunity to cultivate the deeper meanings of either of these traditions. Some of the friends attending were atheist. I tried to be sensitive to these different perspectives on life.

This service was held in the church that had sponsored the family as refugees. A couple dozen people were present: two clergy, several

doi:10.1300/5590_07

church members active in refugee work, the family, and a few friends. The bulletin had Ahmed's picture on the front and a picture of him and his family on the back along with a brief reflection on his life. The order of service and the litany were printed in English and Bosnian, since the family knew almost no English. A translator stood next to the officiant for the entire service.

OPENING PRAYER

"Eternal God, You are known to us by many names; Truth, or Spirit, or Lord. No words can fully describe You. We also use different symbols to describe Your relation to us. For some You are as master and king, striving to bring peace and justice to a torn and shattered world; for some You are as a father, supporting His children in these the hardest times they may ever have to live; for others, You are even as a mother, bringing comfort and nurture.

"The things we most want to say cannot be put into words. We know that You hear those prayers also, the aching in our hearts, the tears in our eyes, the sobbing that lies just beneath the surface. So come to us with strength and love on this day. Amen."

BIOGRAPHICAL STATEMENT
AND OPENING COMMENTS

"We are here today to honor and celebrate the life of Ahmed Cizmak, and to stand together with his family in this time of grief. The family circle is broken. Also broken is their one link to their homeland—a homeland of familiar scenery, familiar homes, familiar smells, familiar voices, and even the familiar chirping of the birds.

"This is too much for any family to bear alone. So we, as a caring community, are here to stand with you in support and love.

"Danka [the wife] now has primary responsibility for two growing sons. May she find the help and friendship she needs.

"Dragen [the elder son] will soon be a man. May he find guidance in a world that is often hostile to human values.

"Ado [the younger son], who is young, will only slowly realize what has happened. May he find support and wisdom.

"Zlydko and Anna [Ahmed's parents] have suffered a loss that nothing can replace. May they find comfort and strength.

"Grief is something you never really get over. You only revisit it in different ways. It is our prayer today that as you, Ahmed's family, visit and revisit your memories and your grief, you will do so with an awareness that God is with you, and that in our own ways, we are with you."

LITANY

The purpose of a litany is to acknowledge both evil and good, both suffering and healing. The leader should be the one to speak the words of anguish and doubt; the people can then speak of support and hope. The process of the litany should be from darkness into light, from despair to hope. The responses of the people should be in their native language. Ideally, the whole service should be in the native language of the participants.

A litany is like a series of questions and answers. The questions are those raised by suffering and despair; the answers point beyond the anguish of the moment and to the deeper realities of life that are symbolized by God.

LEADER: We come together today to honor the memory of Ahmed Cizmak, killed in the senseless cruelty of war. We are also here to honor and support his family in the inexpressible grief that tears at the depth of their hearts.

PEOPLE: Hear our anguished prayers, O God.

LEADER: We are here in the presence of all that is sacred to bear witness to tragedy and loss, to sorrow and heartache.

PEOPLE: Draw near to us, O God, that we may feel Your presence in the midst of our grief.

LEADER: We bring to this moment our bewilderment and doubt. We don't understand how something like this could happen. How can we go on in the face of this tragedy?

PEOPLE: When there are no answers, O God, let us feel Your compassion.

LEADER: We are here to grieve, to weep the tears of desolation and bereavement.

PEOPLE: Be with us in our sorrow.

LEADER: We are here to say NO to war, and to violence, and to cruelty, and to revenge.

PEOPLE: Enable us to see beyond the suffering of this moment.

LEADER: We are here also to say YES to life and to love, even in the midst of the bitterest evil.

PEOPLE: Grant us, O God, a deeper courage, that we may find hope, and may live.

MOMENTS OF APPRECIATION

Before the service, each family member was invited to write three letters, addressed to the deceased. The first is a letter of appreciation, in which some happy memory is remembered. Tell them that they will be invited (not required) to read aloud *only one* portion of that letter. The rest is absolutely private and will never be seen by anyone.

The second letter is a letter of regrets, things you wish you had done differently in relation to the deceased. Ask his forgiveness where that is appropriate.

The third is a letter of resentments. No human relationship is perfect, and the deceased needs your forgiveness also. Mention some incident that will characterize all the things for which he needs forgiveness. Remove the stones from your heart, and express them in a letter. Fold the letters, hold them together with tape and number each letter I, II, or III. If some family members do not wish to write letters, ask them to fold blank pieces of paper and number them.

At this point in the service, the officiant will invite people to read aloud sections from the *first* letter only. The officiant will then gather these first letters together, take them to a special place, and bury them with a brief prayer.

Prayer

In this prayer, the deceased should be referred to in the same terms as he was described in the biographical statement.

"Now Ahmed, lover of nature, man of peace, faithful friend, devoted father, and loving husband, rest in peace, and in the safety of our memories. Amen."

The officiant will now collect the other letters, those expressing regrets and resentments. They are taken to a different place and burned, with an appropriate prayer, such as this.

Prayer

"As these letters release their contents into the air, so do we let go of the feelings that were expressed in them. In the burning of these letters, we commit all resentments and regrets into Your hands, O God. Amen."

CLOSING PRAYER

"Loving God, we now commit to your care the memory of Ahmed Cizmak, knowing that You will remember him for all that was good and loving; and forgive him for what was not. We commit ourselves also to Your care. May we know that in the deepest places of our heart, that is where You meet us. Deeper than our sorrow, deeper than our bereavement, deeper than our rage, deeper even than our doubt, You speak to us with support and compassion. May we feel Your presence now and always. So dismiss us now with peace. Amen."

After the service, the group gathered for refreshments. At one point, Danka said to the group, in very broken English, "When I first came to this country, I had only my children. Now I have my children and you."

Later, she told a friend, "Today I finished something I thought could never be finished."

Chapter 7

A Funeral for a Prodigal Son

Winston was the second son of a Presbyterian minister in a small town. His older brother was a rather typical older brother—a high achiever, very responsible, the apple of his mother's eye. All of his life, success had come easily to him. Winston's two younger brothers were also good students and a credit to the family.

Winston had been a troublemaker from as early as anyone could remember. He was a difficult baby, a difficult toddler, a difficult youngster, a difficult teenager. He seemed to be deliberately flaunting his family's values. Father tried to stand up for him, but Mother was increasingly critical and alienated.

When he was seventeen, after flunking out of two different drug treatment programs, he stole money from the family and ran away from home. No one in his family ever saw him alive again.

Twenty years later, the police in a nearby city called to tell them that Winston had been killed in a robbery attempt. The body had been cremated, and the ashes were going to be delivered to the home.

Mother and Father were devastated. Father had clung to the slim thread of hope that Winston would someday change. For his life to be finalized at the point of his rebellion and pathology was an over-whelming grief.

Mother was angry that he had intruded himself into the family again, causing more pain and chaos. She resented having to go to his funeral.

The elder brother was merely indignant at the shame Winston had brought the family. He would not even attend the funeral. The fourth son was much younger than the others and was unaffected by Winston's situation.

I had known the third son and respected him greatly. For the past several years, he had tried to find out where Winston was living so he

doi:10.1300/5590_08

could make contact with him, but to no avail. When he asked me to lead a memorial service, I was honored. I was also very apprehensive about whether I could say anything that might help bring healing.

Before the service, I met with each of the three persons who would be at the interment: the father, the mother, and the third son. Each had a somewhat different perspective of Winston's life. Each had reacted to Winston differently. Each was suffering in a different way.

I asked each of them to write three letters to Winston and seal them in an envelope. The first would simply describe some of the things they remembered about him. My purpose was to allow Winston to come alive for them again. In the second letter, they would tell him they forgave him for all the things he had done. In the third letter, they would ask him to forgive them for things they may have done that had hurt him.

If they did not want to write such letters, that was all right. They could just bring three blank pieces of paper sealed in an envelope.

I wanted to plant some seeds that might someday bear fruit. I wanted to emphasize forgiveness as the appropriate stance to take with Winston's memory. Even blank pieces of paper could elicit thought processes.

I then asked them to bring the sealed envelopes to the memorial service. I also asked that they bring a picture of Winston, which would be placed by the headstone during the service.

In some traditions, the family members each sprinkle a handful or a shovel full of dirt on the coffin. I asked in advance if the family wished to do this, which they did. I also asked if members of the family would like to be the ones who placed in the grave the small wooden box containing his ashes. They wanted to do this also.

This service seemed to be very helpful to the family, so I am reporting it in full.

OPENING PRAYER

"We are here today with great sadness, O God. Of all the different kinds of suffering there are, the pain of disappointment and loss is among the heaviest. A family which has been torn apart suffers terribly, and yearns for some kind of resolution and healing. We know that You are here among us. May we feel Your presence, Your support, Your love. In the name of Christ, Amen."

MEDITATION

"I want to think with you today about a familiar story that Jesus told. It is the parable of the prodigal son. There was a man who had two sons. The older was a high achiever, loyal, responsible, as older brothers often are. He could do no wrong. The younger, perhaps sensing that he could never live up to the standards his brother had set, became the rebel, the troublemaker. Finally he took money from the family and ran away to a foreign country.

"We don't know all the whys of that decision. No one can ever know fully what is in another person's heart. Maybe it was born of anger, or of pride, or of hurt, or of other things. But it was devastating to the family.

"He immersed himself in a lifestyle that would have been abhorrent to his parents. But finally he came to himself, and returned home to be reunited with his family.

"During all that time, his family still lived in the depth of his heart—deep down, obscured by all kinds of destructiveness, but still there. He never forgot them.

"I am convinced that this is true for everyone. At the core is the wish to love and be loved. This can get clouded by all kinds of things, but the core is still there. I think that is why Jesus spoke so often of forgiveness. He asked us to look beneath the debris of life and to focus on the core. At the core of his soul—no matter what else—Winston loved his family.

"It says of the prodigal son that he came to himself, and was reunited with his family. Tragically, that did not happen for Winston. He died before he "came to himself." So we don't know just how he would have come to that realization. We don't know what words he would have said or what things he would have done to reconnect with his family. We don't know those things; we can't know them. So we have to imagine in our hearts how he would have come home when he came to himself.

"One thing we do know. We know that Winston has now encountered God. He has experienced from God whatever judgment was appropriate, whatever healing was needed, and perhaps most important of all, forgiveness. The debris of Winston's life has been dealt with.

"If Winston could come back now, he would have a lot of things to say to each of us here from the stance of his having made peace with

God. Although we can only imagine *how* he would say them, there are some things we *know* he would say. He would affirm his underlying love for his family. He would ask you to forgive him for all the hurts he has caused you. He would tell you that he forgives you for all the things you have done that hurt him.

"But Winston cannot be here in person to say those things. So we have to imagine in our own minds just *how* he would say those things and what he would ask from you.

"In that spirit, I have asked each member of the immediate family to write three letters addressed to Winston. In one of them, I asked you to tell him some of your memories of him. In the next letter, you offer your forgiveness to him. In the final letter, you ask his forgiveness. If you chose not to write anything, that is fine. I just asked that you bring three blank pieces of paper in an envelope. There are some things that just cannot be expressed in words. Since Winston's body was cremated, I think it is appropriate that these letters be burned also, and the ashes interred along with his ashes."

The letters were placed in an appropriate vessel, and lamp oil was poured on them. The letters were carefully lighted with a long-stemmed match. While they were burning, I read the twenty-third Psalm.

CLOSING PRAYER

"Now O Lord, we commit to the earth the remains of Your child, Winston Armistead. We commit his spirit to You. And we commit to You the things in our hearts that pertain to Winston—memories, wishes, prayers. May we take from this place a deep sense of Your presence and Your peace. And let us pray the Lord's Prayer together."

The mother and father lowered the box into the grave, while the third son placed the ashes from the burned letters alongside the box. The three of them placed a shovelful of dirt in the grave. Cemetery employees then finished filling the grave with soil and placed the marker over the spot. After a few minutes, we all departed.

Chapter 8

Forgiving Another Person

A man approaching his retirement years had owned several sailboats in the course of his life. He belonged to a sailing club, where many of the people he met had become close friends. A dream was to own a marina that would throw him in daily contact with people who loved to sail.

When a suitable piece of land on the lake became available, he retired early and invested most of his savings in the pursuit of his dream. He asked his younger brother, whom he had supported emotionally and financially during a divorce, to go into business with him. The elder brother would provide the capital and the overall planning; the younger brother would handle the day-to-day operation.

After two years, they seemed to be doing a good business, but there were no profits. Finally the elder brother had the books audited and discovered that his younger brother had stolen some $80,000. When confronted with this theft, the younger brother indignantly denied it, and said that there was nothing anybody could prove against him. Nevertheless, within a few days he had left everything and moved to another state.

Arthur's first reaction was helpless rage. How could his own brother do this to him? How could he betray his love and his trust like that? The more he thought about it, the angrier he became. After two months, he realized that his resentment had become a burden that was damaging him physically and emotionally. He knew that he if he were to have any peace, he would have to forgive his brother—to let go of the resentment and get on with his life.

But how?

Portions of this chapter are adapted from my book *Becoming a Forgiving Person,* © 2004, Haworth Pastoral Press.

doi:10.1300/5590_09

His pastor suggested that when it felt right to him to take this step, a formal ceremony might address the situation very helpfully. Several principles might be incorporated.

1. The memories that are most easily accessible at any given time are related to the way a person is feeling at that time. When one is angry, one's thoughts are of all the frustrations in life. When depressed, he or she thinks of things in the past that are associated with depression. When a person is happy, he or she has remembers happy times. When someone feels guilty, all of the hurtful things he or she has ever done may come flooding back into consciousness. These memories then reinforce the initial feeling state.

2. When one experiences a rapid shift from one feeling to another, it tends to soften the intensity of the painful feelings.

3. Being free of resentment (or any other painful feeling) is to enter into another state of mind, another perspective on life, another set of feelings and attitudes, another "world." When one envisions some of the details of this world, one is drawn into it.

4. When people are feeling intensely any negative feeling, that feeling is at the core of their identity. "I am an angry person!" or "I am a guilty person!" Part of the growth process is to move these feelings from the core of the personality to the surface. Instead of saying to oneself, "I am an angry person!" one may come to say something like, "I often feel angry."

5. Any intervention needs to start with rapport. The pastor/therapist needs to let the person know he or she really understands the situation and the person's reactions to it. Only then can a pastor offer healing.

6. When overwhelmed by any intensely negative and painful feeling, a person has in a sense disowned some of his or her own strength, envisioning others as having the power to hurt or to judge or to reject. What he or she then experiences is being on the receiving end of those hurts and judgments—these powers—rather than experiencing oneself as a strong and powerful person. To transcend this kind of powerlessness, it is necessary to affirm one's own strength in relation to other people. Forgiving those who have caused hurt is a powerful expression of this strength, and may be a necessary step in any growth process ("Forgive us our debts as we forgive our debtors . . .").

7. When one is oppressed by painful feelings, one feels alienated from other people. So for a ceremony like this, it would be appropriate for Arthur to bring with him one or more people who truly love him and want what is best for him—a spouse, a parent, a best friend, or so forth. When this was suggested to Arthur, he asked his wife to accompany him.

8. Letters can often be utilized to express feelings and attitudes that are difficult to articulate orally. To write something makes it tangible. When the letter is then disposed of, it can feel as though feelings are disposed of also—not perfectly, but perhaps with more of a sense of finality than can be conveyed verbally.

   One woman said it was very helpful to her to write such a letter, addressed to her abusive ex-husband. She wrote it on what she regarded as appropriate writing material and flushed it down the toilet.

   The pastor might suggest that Arthur write two letters. The first would express his indignation, his hate and resentment toward his brother, and the ways he would like to get even with him. He was asked to put as much intensity into his words as he could.

   The second letter was Arthur's vision of his future *after* he had forgiven his brother: how his stress level would be different, how he would be sleeping, what his energy level would be, what kinds of things would he be enjoying, how he would be relating to family and friends, how he would handle it when he thought of his brother.

9. Speaking a person's name conveys understanding, rapport, and support.

A ceremony such as this should not be rushed. It should be done only when Arthur feels ready to move on.

OPENING PRAYER

"Loving God, we are so often held in the grip of forces over which we seem to have no control—like the grip of hurt and resentment. We are often powerless to prevent another's abuse of us, and feel helpless—sometimes a helpless rage. The chains of helplessness and bitterness easily imprison us, and to forgive seems impossible. Often it really is necessary to 'let goods and kindred go.' So we turn to You, Who came to set Your people free. You have forgiven us, and in Your strength we too may forgive, and be free of the burden of resentment. So touch our lives here today, that we may find peace. In the name of Christ, Amen."

LITANY

LEADER: Loving God, You have come into the turmoil of our world that we may feel your presence even in our struggles.

RESPONDENTS: Lord, hear the prayers of our neediness.

LEADER: You have come to us when we have been abused and betrayed.

RESPONDENTS: Lord, hear the prayers of our pain and confusion.

LEADER: Lord, You come to us when we have suffered great loss and betrayal.

RESPONDENTS: Lord, hear the prayers of our grieving.

LEADER: You have come to sustain us when our tomorrows seem bleak and empty.

RESPONDENTS: Lord, hear the prayers of our fear.

LEADER: You have come to lead us into realities that are deeper than abuse and loss.

RESPONDENTS: Lord, hear the prayers of our hope.

LEADER: You have come to bring us the strength and courage to forgive.

RESPONDENTS: Lord, hear the prayers of our determination.

LEADER: You come to lead us into the light of renewal and life.

RESPONDENTS: Lord, hear the prayers of our hearts.

PRAYER OF CONFESSION

"Eternal and loving God, Who loves us and values us no matter what we have done, we open our hearts to You. We acknowledge the resentments that bind us and hold us in their grasp. We have focused on the negative rather than the positive. We have been at odds with people who are important to us. We have waited for the other person to take the first step. We have withheld our forgiveness, waiting for apologies. We have unrealistically demanded fairness and justice.

"We come to You because in relation to us, You have done what we could not do. You have forgiven. So open our hearts to Your grace, that we may be freed from the resentments that oppress us. In the name of Christ, Amen."

GUIDED MEDITATION

"I would like to invite you, Arthur, to hold your wife's hand, and feel her support during this time of difficult transition. And now let yourself focus inwardly. Put yourself in the presence of a person or persons who truly love you and want what is best for you—perhaps your wife, perhaps a parent, perhaps God—someone who will support you in your efforts to be the kind of person you really want to be. Take a few seconds to put yourself in that scene, and to feel its goodness."

(Pause.)

"Now I would like for you to shift your awareness. Put yourself back in the situation in which you realized your brother had betrayed you. Feel again the hurt and rage of that betrayal. Remember those days when it seemed that your only companion was your hatred and resentment. Feel the tension in your muscles, the clenching of your fists, the determination in your heart to make him hurt as much as you have been hurt. Let yourself feel the passion for revenge."

(Pause.)

"Now let your awareness shift back to the persons who love you and support you. Look into their eyes and hearts. Feel their caring for you, the comfort, the assurance that no matter how anyone else treats you, you are not diminished in their eyes."

(Pause.)

"Now shift back again to the scene of the betrayal. Feel again the shame and humiliation of being treated like that. You did not deserve that."

(Pause.)

"Now open your imagination again to those who will totally support you."

(Pause.)

"Now visit again the situation in which you realized you had been taken advantage of. Many things can be learned from a painful experience like this—things about you, things about life. I would like for you to focus on the learnings that can come from this. You might realize in a deeper way, for instance, that your control of any situation is very limited. You cannot make people be as you want them to be. You might learn about your own naïveté, or your wish to be admired and appreciated. You might learn many other things that can be very valuable to you."

(Pause.)

"Now return to your awareness of those who love you. Focus on things that really matter to you, things that give meaning to your life, things that transcend all the offenses. Feel the warmth of those who love you. Feel their support in leaving behind the pain of betrayal. Feel the presence of God, who is the ground of all forgiveness. Then let your anger transform itself into an affirmation, 'I did not deserve to be treated that way! I am worthy of being treated decently!' Keep saying that until it sinks deep into your consciousness. 'I am worthy of being treated decently!'

"Since this is just an experiment, there is nothing to lose by trying something different. Bring into this scene the person who has so offended you. Feel the support of those who love you; feel your own strength in relation to the person who hurt you. Now tell this person, 'I forgive you. I will pray for you.' You don't need to be wholehearted about it. You don't need to notice if these words have any effect at all on the other person. You are doing this for you, not him. Be aware of how it feels to you to say these words.

(Pause.)

"In the name of Christ, Amen."

At this point, the pastor asks Arthur for the letter expressing his hatred and resentment. Arthur is asked to tear the paper to shreds and put the pieces in a trash can. The pastor says to Arthur that as the letter is disposed of, his own anger and hate can be disposed of also. They can go with the letter into the trash can.

The pastor then asks Arthur for the letter describing his vision of a new future. The pastor places the letter in Arthur's hand, places his or her own hand atop the letter, and prays: "O Lord, bless this letter, and bring its vision into being." The pastor then asks Arthur to keep the letter in a safe place as a reminder of the new beginnings that have been affirmed here today.

BENEDICTION

"And now may the Lord bless you and keep you . . ."

Chapter 9

Forgiving Oneself

Florence thought of herself as a very good nurse: bright, conscientious, caring. One morning, she noticed that her husband seemed to be in some distress. When she asked him about it, he said he had been having abdominal pain for the past few days. This morning, it seemed to be worse. As he talked, a spasm of pain racked his body. He doubled over, face ashen, hands trembling, sweat forming on his forehead. Florence rushed him to the doctor's office, just a short distance from their home.

The doctor was very busy that morning. He took a quick look at Carl and said that he seemed to have the flu. He asked them to wait in a treatment room while his nurse took vital signs.

As a good nurse, Florence knew it was not the flu. It was obviously a serious problem—perhaps even appendicitis. But she could not convince the doctor that her husband was seriously ill and needed immediate attention.

As a nurse, she had been taught always to defer to the doctor. That was a recurrent theme in her training. Besides, that was her own personality style. She found it very difficult to stand up for her own convictions and wishes. So instead of walking out of the doctor's office and going straight to the hospital, she waited and waited and waited. Finally some twenty minutes later, with her husband visibly worse, she took him to the hospital, where they did emergency surgery. Carl survived the surgery, but his system had been seriously weakened. After a couple of days, he took a turn for the worse and lapsed into a coma.

When Florence saw him, she knew he was going to die. She also knew that the time she had wasted in the doctor's office was partly—

Some of the material in this chapter is adapted from my book *Becoming a Forgiving Person,* © 2004, Haworth Pastoral Press.

doi:10.1300/5590_10

maybe largely—responsible for the coma. If she had only had enough initiative and courage, Carl would not now be dying. How could she ever forgive herself?

One friend tried to minimize her responsibility. How can a wife who is overwhelmed with anxiety be expected to make appropriate evaluations and decisions? It was a tragedy, not a crime. It was not something for which she should blame herself. When stressed out, she was just not herself, not the person who usually handles things so well.

Another friend pointed out that other people were more to blame than she was. Carl waited several days before telling her about his pain. Was that his pride, his macho stance? Even if he had sought medical treatment at the very first sign of pain, there is no guarantee he would have lived.

It was partly the doctor's fault. He was the authority. He should have taken charge of the situation immediately. He had no right to dismiss her concern simply because she was distraught.

The hospital may have been partly responsible. Who knows what mistakes or oversights might have occurred? If Carl's condition had been monitored more carefully, might not that have made a difference?

Florence dismissed all of these as rationalizations. She could not dismiss from her mind the conviction that her weakness, her characterological defects, had in effect killed her husband.

For a long time, she looked for ways to atone for this terrible thing. But how? There was no way she could make it up to him or to their family. No restitution was possible. She couldn't fill his shoes as a father to their children. She was already a devoted mother, and did not know what more she could do.

On the other hand, she knew she could not carry this guilt for the rest of her life, or she would destroy her family and herself. She had very little energy or inclination to engage her children. What value could there be in punishing herself so severely, or in suppressing all pleasure and satisfaction?

Florence's friends were trying to restore her innocence, to tell her in various ways that it was not her fault. Florence knew she was not innocent. She was a flawed, defective human being. Nothing could change that, nothing could restore her innocence. She needed—she desperately wanted—to forgive herself. But she had no idea how to accomplish that.

Guilt and shame are not uncommon in our world. Some of it is unrealistic, such as committing one's parents to a nursing home, or losing one's job in a recession, or not being able to stop one's parents from divorcing. But much guilt and shame stem from times when one knows that one has really hurt other people—or oneself. No amount of rationalization can negate that reality.

Forgiveness alone is usually not enough. Guilt for what one has *done* is usually integrally related to shame over who one *is*—"I am ashamed that I am the kind of person who could have done these hurtful things."

Guilt focuses on offenses one has committed and the consequences that might follow. When I feel guilty, I recognize that I have lost favor with the ones I have hurt. I anticipate their criticism and punishment, but I still have a relationship with the them. We may be "separated," but we are not "divorced."

Shame is somewhat different. It focuses not so much on what I have done but on who I am. A person can be shamed in ways that have nothing to do with guilt or even imperfection. For example, children who have been abused—especially those who have been sexually abused—often carry a deep sense of shame into their adult lives. Dostoevski described one woman who felt she was merely a rag on which men wiped off their lust. The resulting feeling was a deep sense of shame: "If you really knew me, you would not want to have anything to do with me. I am so unacceptable I don't deserve to exist."

Guilt and shame certainly overlap in many ways. Perhaps all guilt carries with it some sense of shame. But the difference in emphasis suggests that much of what we call guilt might be thought of more accurately as shame. Florence certainly experienced both.

For this ceremony, Florence was asked to write two letters to herself. The first would express the ways she condemns herself. Let her identify with this critical part of herself and write out the condemnation as elaborately as she can. The second letter is a sketch of the future that will be hers after she has forgiven herself: relations with her children and her friends, activities that will enrich her life, things that will bring a smile to her face, what she will do with her leisure time, and where she will go on vacations. Make sure this letter is at least as long as the first.

She was also encouraged to bring with her someone whom she totally trusted—her mother, in this case.

OPENING PRAYER

"Loving God, You know us better than we ourselves. You know the inner places of our hearts and lives. You know the complex feelings that drive us. You know the dark places in our hearts, our weaknesses, our failures. We come into Your presence today with humility and confidence as we ask for Your healing. We seek the assurance of Your love and forgiveness that enables us to love and accept ourselves. We pray for Florence, that the terrible burdens she carries may be eased, the bonds that have paralyzed her may be broken, and that light may shine into the darkness that has engulfed her. Let the despair and loneliness be lifted. In the name of Christ, Amen."

PERSONAL AFFIRMATION

LEADER: Florence, you come here today knowing that you contributed to the death of your husband, your children's father. You come carrying a deep sense of guilt and shame and unworthiness. So I ask you to consider carefully and prayerfully the following questions. Do you acknowledge that you are a flawed and imperfect human being, and that you always will be?

RESPONDENT: I do.

LEADER: And do you feel a great sense of guilt and shame about your flaws?

RESPONDENT: Yes, I do.

LEADER: When you feel guilt and shame, does that help you to be a better mother to your children?

RESPONDENT: No, it does not.

LEADER: Do guilt and shame help you to be a more kind and loving person?

RESPONDENT: No, they do not.

LEADER: When the feelings of guilt and shame come upon you, does that help you to be a more spiritual person?

RESPONDENT: No , it does not.

LEADER: When you step into those feelings of guilt and shame, do you feel closer to God?

RESPONDENT: No, I do not.

LEADER: If your husband were here, would he want you to feel guilty and shameful for your deficiencies—even to those that contributed to his death?

RESPONDENT: No, he would not.

LEADER: Do your children want you constantly to remind yourself of your failings?

RESPONDENT: No, they do not.

LEADER: If a friend or family member were in your situation, would you want him or her to carry the same burden that you carry?

RESPONDENT: No, I would not.

LEADER: And do you now, in the presence of God, solemnly distance yourself from all guilt and shame, and accept the love and forgiveness of God?

RESPONDENT: Yes, with God's help I do.

LEADER: Do you now solemnly promise that when these painful feelings visit you,* you will remind yourself that God has forgiven you and God loves you, and that you will then turn from those unnecessary feelings and get on with the day's activities?

RESPONDENT: Yes, with God's help I will.

LEADER: Let us pray together the Lord's Prayer . . .

LITANY

LEADER: Loving God, You come into the turmoil of our inner world to bring release and healing.

RESPONDENTS: Lord, hear the prayers of our neediness.

---

*Notice the progression from "a flawed and imperfect person" [rapport] to "when these painful feelings visit you" [a new future].

LEADER: You come to us in the face of all our imperfections. You come to us knowing that we have hurt other people who are important to us.

RESPONDENTS: Lord, hear the prayers of our confession.

LEADER: You come to us when we are overwhelmed with guilt and shame.

RESPONDENTS: Lord, hear the prayers of our yearning to be free.

LEADER: You come to sustain us when our tomorrows seem bleak and empty.

RESPONDENTS: Lord, hear the prayers of our fear.

LEADER: You come to lead us to the place where we can have pity on ourselves, where we can forgive ourselves.

RESPONDENTS: Lord, hear the prayers of our hope.

LEADER: You come to bring us the strength and courage to live in spite of all our flaws and our faults.

RESPONDENTS: Lord, hear the prayers of our determination.

LEADER: You come to lead us into the light of renewal and life.

RESPONDENTS: Lord, hear the prayers of our hearts.

PRAYER OF CONFESSION

"Eternal and loving God, Who loves us and values us no matter what we have done, we open our hearts to You. We confess the terrible ways we have hurt those we love. We confess the difficulty in forgiving ourselves. We confess the bonds of guilt and shame that enslave us. We confess that we have submitted to darkness, and that our energy for living has been consumed by this darkness. We have been so focused on our own needs for love and forgiveness that we have neglected to forgive those who have hurt us. So open our hearts to Your grace, that that which is past may be laid aside, and we may find peace and confidence and strength. In the name of Christ, Amen."

GUIDED MEDITATION

"I would like to invite you, Florence, to hold your mother's hand, and feel her support for you during this time of difficult transition."

(Pause.)

"And now let yourself focus inwardly. Put yourself in the presence not only of your mother, whose hand you hold, but also of another person or persons who truly love you and want what is best for you— perhaps your husband, perhaps parents or friends, perhaps God— those who will support you in your efforts to move beyond the paralysis of guilt and shame, who will support your commitment to being the kind of person you really want to be. Take a few seconds to put yourself in that scene and to feel its goodness."

(Pause.)

"Now, Florence, I would like for you to shift your awareness. Put yourself back in the hospital when you realized that Carl was going to die and that you were partly responsible. Feel again that terrible feeling in the pit of your stomach, that wish that you might just disappear, that fear that you will never be able to look anyone in the eye again. Feel again the full burden of guilt and shame."

(Pause.)

"Now let your awareness shift back to the persons who love you and support you. Look into their eyes and hearts. Feel their caring for you, their assurance that no matter what you have done, you are truly loved and appreciated. Let yourself feel their warm embrace, and know that nothing can separate you from their love and commitment."

(Pause.)

"Now shift back again to the scene at the hospital and feel again the intensity of guilt you have been carrying."

(Pause.)

"Now open your imagination again to those who will totally love you and support you."

(Pause.)

"Now visit the hospital again. You know that you are now responsible for the well-being of your children as well as for yourself. You do not want to make mistakes in the future. So this might a good time to look within yourself, calmly, intellectually, and objectively, to identify some areas of growth for yourself. You might think of some of the things that will nurture that growth. Think of the people who will be there for you, to help bring that future into being. Project yourself now into that future and experience satisfaction, knowing that there really are new beginnings."

(Pause.)

"Now return, Florence, to those who love you, especially to your husband, Carl. Be aware that the things that really matter in life—love and joy and purpose, the things that give meaning to your life—these are still available to you. Feel the warmth of those who love you. Feel their support in leaving behind the pain of your mistakes, no matter how tragic they may have been. Feel the presence of God, who is the ground of all life.

"Since this is just an experiment, Florence, there is nothing to lose by trying out something a bit different. Feel again the support of those who love you; feel your own strength in relation to your future. Let the condemning part of you face the guilty part of you, and say to her, 'I truly forgive you. I want you to have a good life.'"

(Pause.)

"In the name of Christ, Amen."

❧

At this point, the pastor asks Florence for the letter condemning herself. She is asked to tear the paper to shreds and put the pieces in a large aluminum bowl. A bit of fuel oil is poured on the pieces and they are burned. The pastor talks softly while the letter is burning.

"As this letter is consumed by fire, it is transformed into smoke and gas, and dissipated into the atmosphere. The feelings that were expressed in this letter—guilt, shame, despair, helplessness—these too can be consumed and dissipated, and you can experience freedom. In the name of Christ, Amen."

The pastor then asks for the letter describing her future. He or she places it in Florence's hand, places his or her own hand atop the letter, and prays: "O Lord, bless this letter, and bring its vision into being." The pastor then asks Florence to keep the letter in a safe place as a reminder of the new beginnings that have been affirmed here today.

CLOSING PRAYER

"Florence, as a minister of Christ, I am responsible for saying to you the things I think Jesus would say to you. In that spirit, I reverently declare to you that all your sins are forgiven, all your shame is set aside.

"Now, O Lord, we commit ourselves to You—with all the failures of the past, and all the commitments to the future. And now may the Lord bless you and keep you . . ."

Chapter 10

Addressing Children's Phobias

Many children are frightened of monsters. They hear them in their closet or under their bed; they see their shadows on the wall; strange smells fill the room. Parents try to assure them that there is no such thing as a monster, but these assurances fall on deaf ears. The monsters are real to the children.

At least two things contribute to children's phobias. The first is their general sense of helplessness in the world. Children are small; everyone else seems gigantic. They are weak; everyone and everything else seems much stronger. They are surrounded by things they cannot control. When they go to bed, they face the world alone and may feel that their parents have abandoned them.

Monsters can easily symbolize this threatening world. In the child's mind, monsters are huge and malevolent. It is hard enough to deal with something (or someone) you can see. It is even more distressing to have to deal with something that is invisible, that is known only by shadows and eerie sounds.

A second source of phobias may be an aggression that gets disowned. All human beings manifest some kind of aggression, more so in some situations than others. Children too have angry feelings. But if they feel deep inside that they should not have these feelings or let them show, then they may engage in a kind of denial. They disown those feelings in themselves and project the aggression onto something or someone in the outside world. This acknowledges that the aggression is there, but they do not experience it as their own. An extreme form of this is called paranoia. Others (such as monsters) are the ones who are malevolent.

A ceremony to address children's phobias, such as the one presented here, would have several features. It would give the child an activity to do, rather than be passive in the face of threats. It would

doi:10.1300/5590_11

give the child a sense of power and control, as in passing judgment on the monster and yelling at him. It would demonsterize the monster in several ways (such as by implying that he still watches cartoons and must obey his mommy). It enlists an adult and other family members as allies and protectors. It utilizes something tangible with magic powers. It introduces an element of playfulness, which is incompatible with fear. It expresses aggression as an appropriate part of the child's own personality.

It might be argued that this approach gives reality to the monsters, which is not what you want. But the monsters are real to the child; they are a child's language for expressing anxiety. To address a child's fears meaningfully, you must use a child's language and a child's logic, not adult language and logic.

Before the ceremony, purchase an aerosol room freshener and paint dramatic designs on it with vivid colors—especially red, a color often associated with anger. The aerosol has now become "Monster Repellant."

The afternoon before the ceremony, use your ingenuity, with the assistance of the child, to make some Monster Cookies. You can bake these or purchase them. Cut the cookies into appropriate shapes, and decorate them accordingly.

Just before bedtime, the family will gather together in the child's bedroom. Since one purpose of this ceremony is to give the child a sense of control, ask the child where each person should stand. Then have the child describe the monster by answering some of your pointed questions, similar to the examples given here.

"Is this a boy monster or a girl monster [notice that the monster is described as being a child]? What color is it? Is it pink? Or maybe orange? Or maybe pink with great big yellow polka-dots [notice the use of 'harmless' colors]? What color do you think it is?"

"How big do you think this monster is? Do you think he would fit in a thimble? Or maybe a cup? Or do you think he might possibly be big enough to fit in a cereal bowl [these questions define the monster as small]?"

"Do you think this monster is fat, or is he skinny?"

"What about his voice? Do you think he has a southern accent [which the adult will mimic]? Is his voice high pitched [demonstrate], or is it very high pitched and squeaky [demonstrate]?"

"What do you think he likes to eat? Does he like Cheerios? And does he like Twinkies? And what about broccoli? Do you think he likes broccoli?"

If the child answers these questions in ways that suggest the monster really is big and strong, tell him that is fine, because the Monster Repellant spray always works better the bigger the monster is.

At this point, explain the procedure to the child.

First, if the family is at all religious, they might open with a prayer: "Almighty God, we know that you are stronger than any monster. We ask you to let [child's name] know that you guard this room and protect him forever! Amen."

Next, everybody yells at the monster while stomping their feet. An adult may read each line softly, and have the family repeat it loudly.

> Monster, Klopster, you are bad,
> You are banished from this pad.
> Monster, Klopster, you will see,
> It is time for you to flee!

Then the child will spray the Monster Repellant every place he or she thinks there might be a monster: in the closets, around the windows, in drawers of the furniture, under the beds, behind pictures, etc. With each spray, the child might say something such as, "Be gone, Monster!"

Finally, an adult may yell at the monster again, or lead the child in doing so: "You're a bad monster. If you ever come here again, we'll tell your mommy on you, and she won't let you watch cartoons for a whole week!"

The can of Monster Repellant is left prominently on the dresser, and the family retires to the kitchen to demolish the monster cookies. Encourage the child to destroy the monster by destroying the cookies [a way of expressing aggression]. If the child is afraid the monster will be mad, tell him or her that whatever power the monster had is now in the cookies. When you eat them, that power becomes yours, and helps you become big and strong.

PART II:
THE LIFE CYCLE

Chapter 11

Marriage

PREMARITAL CONSULTATION

There are several different approaches to premarital counseling, and many clergy are requiring this as part of the wedding package. As a pastoral counselor, I am not the minister of a church, and so most of the people who ask me to perform a wedding are referred by friends or by wedding centers. If I require too much in the way of premarital counseling, most of the couples will simply look for another minister.

Most of the people I see for weddings have their act together fairly well. The fact that I am a minister screens out most who don't. I am sure that my insisting on premarital consultation screens out others. Also, I tell them I am very hesitant to perform a wedding for people who are under twenty-one, or who have been involved for less than a year, or who have been divorced for less than a year. Marriage is difficult enough in the best of circumstances without entering it naively. If I am going to bless someone's marriage, I want to be able to do it wholeheartedly.

I tell the couple that I like to see them for one hour of premarital consultation. I use this word rather than "counseling" because it is less threatening. I say something such as this:

"I think all relationships have issues. But they are different from one couple to another. If you can get a sense of what your issues are likely to be, you are a step ahead. So when an issue arises, you can say to yourselves, 'Oh, that's what Henry was talking about!' rather than saying, 'There's something wrong with us.'"

"Also, this gives me an opportunity to know you a little bit. I don't want just to perform a ceremony; I want to bless your marriage, and I can't do that if I don't have a 'feel' for who you are."

doi:10.1300/5590_12

There are two basic questions that should be asked of any relationship: "Is this relationship worthwhile?" and "Is this relationship realistic?" The worthwhileness has to do with the romance, delight, and passion that bring people together. It is wonderful, and it is all they are aware of for the first year or so of their relationship—the honeymoon period. During this time they close their eyes to things that might be troubling to them.

The realistic questions have to do with their ability to share responsibility and to resolve conflict gracefully. Are their worldviews compatible? Do they make small talk easily? Will they refrain from trying to change the other person?

Things they like about their relationship will probably get better; the things they don't like are guaranteed to get worse. If they cannot accept that, they should not marry.

In the long run, I think the realistic factors are the most important. Romance may be wonderful, but if you cannot resolve conflicts, your relationship will disintegrate.

❧

During the session, I focus on three areas.

The first area I discuss is how people's worldviews differ. This is a very broad term, encompassing such issues as how people spend money, how they deal with in-laws, how much and what kind of romance is appropriate, who initiates talk about issues of concern, who apologizes first, who is supposed to be the first to say "I love you," and so forth. Each person thinks his or her worldview is the only one that any normal person could possibly entertain, and may be totally bewildered or even offended to find out the spouse is different.

Two contrasting worldviews are particularly difficult. One person may be a neatnik and the other a slob. Each is absolutely convinced his or her style is right. The other is the level of animation. If one is a high-energy person and the other very laid back, there is likely to be much conflict until each gives up trying to change the other.

The second area concerns one of the sources of our worldviews: sibling positions in their families of origin. It is with our brothers and sisters that we pick up our basic style (worldview) of relating to our peers. Somebody that grows up in one sibling position tends to develop one kind of style; someone who grows up in another tends to

-develop a different style. These different styles may mesh smoothly, or they may mesh only with difficulty. You can deal with this better if you know about it in advance.

A body of literature is now available on this subject. I like Walter Toman's book *Family Constellation* (1993). It provides a gentle and forgiving means of addressing marital issues.

After discussing the sibling relations and how that impacts their lives together, I then talk about the ways men and women tend to communicate differently. There is a body of literature on this area also. The best book I know, and which I give to all couples, is Deborah Tannen's *That's Not What I Meant* (1986). Dr. Tannen's book *You Just Don't Understand* (1990) is also excellent.*

I give every couple a sheet of paper with some questions for personal reflection. This is for them, not for me. At the top of one side of the paper I ask: "What are your wishes and dreams for your marriage? What mutual goals will help unite you? What will help create a sense of 'we' and 'us' rather than just 'you' and 'me'?" The rest of the page is blank for their answers.

On the back of this piece of paper, there is room for the groom and the bride to respond to some more questions:

"What are some mistakes your parents made in their marriages? What personal characteristics contributed to these mistakes? In what ways do you have some of those same characteristics? How will you try to avoid the mistakes your parents made? Knowing yourselves, what are some mistakes you are likely to make in your marriage? What steps can you take, now and later, to avoid or at lease minimize those mistakes?"

At the end of the premarital session, unless they are so screwed up that I cannot in good conscience perform the wedding, I will always say something positive to them. I may comment on their honesty, their maturity, their ease in communicating, or so forth. I want them to leave with the idea that they have a relationship that is worthy of their wholehearted investment.

---

*Dr. Tannen also has other books on this. John Gray's best-selling book *Men Are from Mars, Women Are from Venus* (1992) popularizes some of Dr. Tannen's work. If you can get beyond the cutesy-pie style of this book, you will find some good material in it.

At the rehearsal, I give them four identical 3″ × 5″ laminated cards on which are printed some excerpts from the wedding service. These can be used as bookmarks, or held on the refrigerator door with magnets. These four cards are first printed on one sheet of paper and then cut to size. I use twelve-point italic type, with each line centered, and use very nice paper purchased from an art supply store. The text is all loaded on my computer, so only the names and dates need to be changed for each couple. The lamination is done for about a dollar at an office supply store.

names

date
. . . leaving a trail of happiness,
knowing that in each day,
we are creating memories
that will be part of our lives
forever.

I will honor and support you
in all your endeavors,
and I will do my best
to bring laughter, joy, and purpose
to our life together.

. . . to enjoy you
for what you are,
and to forgive you
for what you are not.

MINISTERING TO NERVOUS BRIDES

A ceremony addresses two facets of all transitions in life: the reality of loss, and an affirmation of one's commitment to a new future. There are losses in a marriage, although they are in the background, implicit rather than explicit. There is a loss of independence and a commitment to something from which one cannot easily extricate oneself. There is also—at least in first marriages—a realization that one's childhood is truly and finally past. These losses are usually not addressed in a wedding service.

In a typical wedding, the participants (and/or their parents) invest a tremendous amount of money, time, energy, and feeling in planning for the happy event. Everyone wants it to go smoothly. But the very importance of the wedding creates anxiety—sometimes a debilitating anxiety. Most often, it is exhibited by the bride, who is afraid she will faint (or vomit). Friends and family tell her there is nothing to be worried about—which of course makes things worse. Not only must she cope with her own anxiety, she must now deal with people who are telling her there is something wrong with her for being nervous.

Part of my responsibility as a minister is to help allay people's anxieties. These are some of the things I do.

In my first contact with the couple, and also at the rehearsal, I tell people that it is very bad luck for everything to go smoothly at a wedding. That would not be true to life. I then tell them that no matter what goes awry, it is my responsibility to cover. That doesn't mean I can always do it, but it is my responsibility. If anyone is going to look stupid, it will be me.

The main distractions during the wedding services are background noises and, for out-of-doors weddings, the weather. I have often said something like this to the guests:

"I want to express my appreciation for the [noise, bad weather, or so forth]. It is a reminder of a fundamental principle of life. Anybody can have a good marriage when everything goes the way you want it to. The challenge of marriage is to live well in spite of life's disappointments and interferences."

No matter what happens, if it is important enough to be noticed, I will comment on it. Candles might not light, someone may faint, the wind may wreak havoc with gowns, hair, bouquets, and so forth. Everything can be described as symbolic.

つ

I always urge people not to have singing *during* the service. People just cannot conceive of how long a song can be while you are standing up there. One couple disregarded this admonition. The song dragged on and on. Both bride and groom were so nervous they were shaking.

Knowing that one way to ease people's anxieties is to talk to them, I embarked on a long speech. I began with a whispered question. "Have you started a scrapbook of embarrassing memories to show your children?"

They had not.

"I think this would be an excellent place to begin. Write down how nervous you both are, and all the things that have gone wrong in the preparation for this wedding. I guarantee that your children will appreciate it."

I then asked if their parents had had a scrapbook about their embarrassing memories.

They had not.

"Then you can do something for your children that your parents didn't know to do for you."

I kept on talking in this vein until finally the song ended. After the service, both bride and groom thanked me profusely for what I had done.

つ

I tell the bride and groom that I plan to be at the wedding service an hour early. They have enough to worry about without wondering if the minister is going to show up. If for some reason I am not there at least twenty minutes before the time for the wedding, it means something has happened to me. I have been in a serious accident, or dropped dead, or been abducted by aliens from the galaxy Sodium Hydroxide. If that happens, they can call a friend (whose name and number I give) who will fill in for me. Just in case, bring a copy of your wedding service to both the rehearsal and to the wedding.

While you are waiting for the substitute minister to arrive, just go ahead and have the reception first. But don't worry. I'll be there. I have never yet dropped dead or been abducted by aliens.

As soon as I arrive, I will check in with the bride and the groom. About fifteen minutes before the service is to begin, I will check in with the bride again. This is usually when she is the most nervous.

First, I want to undo the pressure that family put on her by telling her not to be nervous. I will tell the bride nonchalantly, "There's absolutely nothing to worry about. Just remember that this is the single most important event in your entire life, and every eye will be on you to evaluate your performance!

"Seriously, if you are concerned about fainting (or vomiting), there is no problem. We can appoint a designated fainter (or puker). The maid of honor is probably the best choice. That's part of her responsibility. And the rule is that only one person is allowed to faint (or puke) during a wedding. If you would rather have someone else be the designated fainter, that is all right. Maybe Mother or Sister would volunteer, but I think the maid of honor is the ideal.

"Of course, if you want to do the fainting yourself, you should make a production out of it. Pick a place where the photographer will be sure to get it on film—like maybe halfway down the aisle. I think it would be better if you faint while you are with your dad rather than when you are with your husband-to-be. And be sure to do it dramatically. Slowly raise the back of your hand to your forehead and moan loudly as you sink slowly to the ground."

One purpose of these apparently strange comments it to give the bride a sense of control. The fear of fainting and/or vomiting is a fear of losing control. A suggestion that at least gives the illusion of control (picking a place to faint) can alleviate the sense of having no control. And humor is always a graceful way to alleviate anxiety.

If the bride is concerned about crying—another situation where she feels out of control—I will try to normalize the crying, and then give her a sense of control relative to it.

Personally, I think it is beautiful when people weep at a wedding. It reflects the importance of this step, and speaks of the depth of their souls they are making available to the other.

I tell the bride that if she weeps, she should embrace her husband-to-be for as long as she wishes. The guests are here to support you, not to witness a performance.

If they do weep during the service, I may whisper to them something like, "That's fine. That's fine. Just take your time. There is no rush. I know how important this is to you."

These simple procedures have a remarkable ability to alleviate anxiety, so the wedding service can be a time of joy and affirmation rather than embarrassment or dread.

THE WEDDING SERVICE

Planning

At our first meeting, I give couples a list of suggestions for the planning of the wedding service, which includes the following two items.

Music

If you are going to have singing, please have it after the mothers are seated, and before any of the wedding party is standing up before the guests. If you have singing during the service, it will sound incredibly long.

Remember that the musicians are working for you, not the other way around. Tell them not only what to play, but also how loudly you want it played. Remind the musicians of this the day of the wedding. I suggest that the bridal march be played softly rather than bombastically. This is an intimate occasion, not a spectacle.

Photographers

Remember that the photographer is working for you! Some photographers get carried away, and do things that are terribly intrusive. One photographer preceded the bride down the aisle, taking pictures. Another walked up and down the central aisle taking pictures of the guests. Another stood next to the minister to take close-ups of the bride and groom.

If this is what you want, fine. It is your wedding. But if you do not like things like that, be sure to tell the photographer *in detail* what you want and what you don't want.

It may seem strange to think of a wedding as a therapeutic ceremony. But it is a wonderful opportunity for teaching. Even though the two people are in a state of blissful indifference to the world of reality, seeds can be planted that may come to fruition at a later date.

When people marry, they tend to have very high expectations of their relationship. They pledge their eternal love to each other and know that life will be wonderful, with few problems. No matter how much they know intellectually that marriage is difficult, in their hearts they *know* they will be the exception. They promise a level of romance and unity that simply cannot be lived out in real life.

But Utopia is never just around the corner. Along with the beauty of their love is the inevitable reality of difference and conflict.

A good wedding ceremony addresses both of these realities. It is a blend of idealism and common sense. It affirms the positive while also recognizing the need for hard work and forgiveness.

An event this important needs to have a certain "heft" in several areas. Weddings usually involve guests, refreshments, music, and flowers as well as a formal ceremony. The ceremony needs to be long enough to do justice to the importance of this transition, and to the enormous time, energy, money, and feelings that have gone into it. Weddings costing $20,000 and more are not uncommon. A six-minute service is simply not enough.

For an average wedding, I like a service fifteen to twenty minutes long. In it, I try to find a happy balance between the beautiful and the practical.

Most (maybe all) religious traditions have evolved wedding services that are more or less standard. I am presenting here only a few comments that may supplement these services. The hypothetical couple are Andrea and Roger. Andrea is a Baptist from Georgia; Roger is Anglican from England. Each has a child from a previous marriage: Andrea's daughter Laura is nine; Roger's son Matthew is eight. Both of the children will be involved in the wedding service and then will be living with them. Roger and Andrea want to have two more children together. Also, each has one much-loved grandfather who is no longer living. They are represented by memorial candles, lit by the mothers when they are seated.

Ceremony Introduction

After the opening remarks, I will ask, "Who represents this woman's family in adding their blessing to this relationship?" After Dad (or Dad and Mother) says "I do," I will ask the same question of the groom's mother (and father). This emphasizes balance and equality in the marriage more than the traditional, "Who gives this woman in marriage?"

Some couples want a special recognition for their parents. "Andrea and Roger want to express to you their parents, their deep appreciation for you, and for the homes you established for them, and for the kinds of marriages you have modeled for them—marriages of commitment, loyalty, and love. They hope to bring into their marriages the qualities they so appreciated in your marriages."

If they have memorial candles, I will say, "Each of us stands in a special place in the flow of life from one generation to another. For you, Andrea and Roger, two grandfathers who are no longer living are represented here by memorial candles and are here in spirit. Other family are here with you also, to celebrate with you, and to bless you in this marriage."

Principles of Marriage

After discussing some principles of marriage, I say to a couple with children from previous relationships: "You each bring with you the experiences of a former marriage, some joyful, some painful. Among the blessings are your children who stand with you today. Your daughter, Andrea, Laura, and your son, Roger, Matthew—they too become part of the life the two of you are building."

A Charge to the Couple

"Andrea and Roger, this is the most sacred commitment you will ever make. There are several principles implicit in this commitment, and I ask you to take these seriously.

"Perhaps most important of all is to treat each other with kindness.

"Don't be content with a life that flows smoothly—no matter how pleasing that life is. You need occasional experiences that are really special, where you put all your ingenuity and creativity to work to create magic for the other person.

"It is important also to enter this marriage unencumbered by the mistakes of the past—either your mistakes or someone else's. So I urge you to forgive everyone who has hurt you, and to let go of all resentment. Forgive yourselves also, so that your mistakes can be sources of learning rather than burdens of guilt.

"I charge you both to understand that you will never get everything you want from a marriage. No one ever does. But if you can cherish the 90 percent that's there, instead of complaining about the 10 percent that's not, you will find the 90 percent can be wonderful. You will never be able to make your partner change, so please don't try. You are each responsible for your own lives. It is up to each of you to make your own lives interesting and worthwhile, and then to share that interest and worthwhileness with each other. Instead of admonishing the other to be more loving and forgiving, you can only initiate your own love, appreciation, and forgiveness. Initiate especially your own ability to deal with adversity gracefully and always remember the old adage: 'If I can prove I'm right, I make things worse.'

"I urge you to say often the words 'I love you.' Usually, these will be a report. But it is especially important to say them when you are not feeling loving toward each other. The words are then a promise, a commitment, a definition of a future that beckons you.

"Many people want to be adored without having to *do* anything. They will just stand there, and the partner will beam at them with delight. This is called the honeymoon of the relationship, and it is wonderful. But honeymoons end. You will then discover that you must go out of your way to meet each other's needs. You can't just be yourself and have a good marriage. It takes compromise.

"It is easy to love someone who thinks you are wonderful, and whom you think is wonderful. But after a year or so—maybe sooner—you will discover that you are both imperfect. The challenge of marriage then begins: to love someone who is imperfect, and more than that, to love someone who knows that you are imperfect.

"By your coming together today in marriage, you are bringing together not only the rich heritages of two different families, but also the traditions of two different nationalities, two different cultures, each with its unique perspectives on life, its priorities, its wisdom. You also bring together two different spiritual traditions, each speaking in its own way of eternal values, of love, and of forgiveness. I charge you today to let those differences enrich your lives, individually and together, understanding that true spirituality is never competitive, but seeks to build up, to enhance, to bring together. As two mighty rivers converge, each bearing the nutrients of its origins, they become together a deeper and richer source of life for all that they touch."

Prayer

"We are grateful, O God, for this happy time together, and for the things that have made this occasion possible. We are grateful for the thousands of influences on their lives that have enabled Roger and Andrea to become the persons they are, and to find and touch and love each other . . ."

Acceptance of Responsibility

After the exchange of responsibility ("Do you Roger, take Andrea . . ."), I will address the guests: "And will you, loved ones and friends, support Roger and Andrea in this marriage, by helping create a world characterized by love and forgiveness? If so, say, 'I do.'"

Comments on Marriage

"Andrea and Roger, you are as two artists, commissioned to create a living canvas of your lives and your relationship. In the living of each day you add form and texture and beauty, creating memories. So paint the scenes of your lives with happiness, anticipating the times when you will look back with pleasure and satisfaction.

"Paint with care your own uniqueness and individuality. Paint the equalities of your relationship with broad strokes, so that you don't contend over trivia. Let the tender colors of your togetherness be clear and strong. Learn how to comfort, without smothering; how to confront, without malice. In every confrontation, always assume the other's motives are benign rather than malicious . . ."

Exchange of Vows

"Roger and Andrea, the vows you now make are based on a fundamental principle of life: people make decisions based on other people's promises. Please don't ever forget that. Your marriage is based on your promises even more than it is on your love."

"I love you, Andrea/Roger, and I take you now to be my beloved wife/husband. I solemnly commit myself, in the presence of God and these friends, to be your loving and faithful husband/wife; through the dark times of life as well as the bright ones, throughout the days of our lives. I will honor and support you in all your endeavors, and I will do my best to bring laughter, joy, and purpose to our life together."

"In addition to the formal vows, Roger and Andrea wanted to say something more personal to each other."

Roger reads from a scroll:

"I am here with you today with a profound sense of humility and gratitude. You are everything I have ever wanted in a partner: you are a kindred spirit, a good friend, easy to be with, generous, honest, spiritual, and obviously beautiful. We have similar tastes and values in practically everything. We make small talk easily, we enjoy being together even when we say nothing. We love to touch and to be touched. We take delight in each other. Even more than my love for you is my conviction that we will have a good life together.

"I can't promise that I will never be petty or irritable or insensitive. But I can promise that I will not blame you for what is wrong with me. I will take your concerns about our relationship seriously. I will not try to change you.

"I will do my best to cultivate a sense of 'we' and 'us' rather than just 'me' and 'you.' I want to regard each day with you as a gift. I will do my best to leave a trail of happiness as our lives progress.

"And so now, with my whole heart, I embrace you as my wife, my beloved, unique to me in all the world."

Andrea then reads from another scroll:

"I too feel a sense of wonder and awe as we stand here to take this step together on our journey. I love the things we share together. I love your playfulness and your gentleness, I love your values and your integrity. I love your laughter, and your way with children. I love you. I share the dream that we will have a good life together.

"I promise to cherish you and nurture you, to take you seriously even when I don't understand, to hold your hand in times of difficulty. I will not try to make you fulfill all my expectations, but will accept you and honor you for who you are. I will always try to be slow to anger and quick to forgive.

"I pledge to you my trust and my loyalty. I will dream with you, and work with you, and love you. I will do my best to make our life together better rather than worse, deep rather than shallow, challenging rather than boring, rich rather than poor, healthy rather than sick, joyful rather than sad.

"I embrace you with love and deepest gratitude: husband, lover, friend, as you are, nothing wanting, nothing changing, my heart's companion and my mind's delight.

"And I marry you with my whole self."

Exchange of Rings

After Andrea and Roger have exchanged rings, I will address the fact that they both have children.

"A marriage is more than just a husband and a wife. A marriage is also the establishing of a family. And your family, Roger and Andrea, includes Laura and Matthew. So it is appropriate that there be a special gift for them also—a way of saying to them, 'We belong together. We are a family.'"

Roger places a ring on Laura's *right* hand. The ring symbolizes that they are a family, not that Laura is a second wife. Andrea gives a wristwatch to Matthew.

Unity Candle

Many couples, especially in a first marriage, like to use the unity candle as part of the ceremony. Traditionally, after the bride and groom have lit the unity candle, they extinguish the individual ones. I strongly oppose this. They are gaining a relationship, not losing their selves.

Closing Prayer

Since Roger and Andrea want to have more children, I suggested that this blessing be added to the closing prayer:

"Now Roger, great-grandson of David Alexander, grandson of George Kendall, son of Robert Alan; and Andrea, great-granddaughter of Catherine Anne, granddaughter of Gladys Louise, daughter of Barbara Gail, from father to son and mother to daughter through the generations, may you be blessed with children and grandchildren and great grandchildren in the flow of life from generation to generation . . ."

Then follows the declaration of marriage, the benediction, and the introduction of the couple.

Chapter 12

Pre- and Postbaptism

Baptism provides a wonderful opportunity for pastoral care for the family. The pastor can visit the family prior to the service and affirm with them their dreams for the child.

This kind of visit also lets the child begin to know the minister and to be comfortable with her (or him): to hear her voice, to feel her touch, to smell her breath. Then when the minister holds the baby for the baptism, she will not be a stranger.

The pastor can also talk with the parents about some principles of child rearing. One of the most important is to raise the child with gentleness and intelligence. A parent should not ask for obedience—that is what you want from your dog. You want a child to cooperate. The task of parenting from this perspective is to avoid the power struggles of trying to make the child obey (in which everyone inevitably loses), and to elicit the child's cooperation. Hopefully, the parent is more intelligent than the child and can think of ways to do this. It is easier if you take a child's objectional behavior as a challenge to your ingenuity rather than to your self-esteem. An adversarial approach to parenting is most unfortunate.

I wish these principles could be incorporated into the formal baptism service. The questions to the parents might include, "Do you covenant with God and this congregation to raise your child with gentleness and forgiveness?" "Do you commit yourselves to avoiding all power struggles?" "Will you seek cooperation from this child rather than obedience?"

Infant baptism presupposes that the family rather than the individual is the basic unit of life. That is difficult for we as Americans to understand. We see the family as a collection of individuals, and it is hard for us to grasp the sense of family unity that exists in most of the rest of the world. To carry that over into our religious life, we think

doi:10.1300/5590_13

that only adults should be baptized. We Americans are all Baptists at heart.

One friend wanted to have a postbaptism party at his home the following Saturday after the church baptism and asked me to write a ceremony for the occasion. Here is part of it:

"A parent's love is a paradox, a mystery.

"It hungers to reach out, to touch and to embrace;

"It also takes pleasure in releasing and standing back.

"It rejoices in the child's successes, but does not shield her from failure.

"It enjoys the child in her, while glimpsing and awakening ever so gently the adult that is also within.

"It gives, and rejoices in the giving, but it does not demand that its gifts be received.

"It is grateful for moments of intimacy, and patient in times of anguish.

"It seeks to love Teresa for what she is, and to forgive her for what she is not."

Following these comments, the vows were said alternately by the father and the mother.

> I, Ned, *and I, Patricia,* do now in the presence of God, *lovingly accept you, Teresa, as our daughter.* And we proudly commit ourselves to being your parents: *To provide for you what you cannot provide for yourself;* to share with you the inner spirit of our lives; *To care for you, no matter what may happen;* [together] To rejoice with you in your world, in your growing, in your loving.

"Let us pray: Loving God, Father, Mother, Friend, and Protector, we are grateful for the privilege of living. We rejoice now in this moment when new life and new relationships are affirmed in Your presence. Grant to Patricia and Ned courage and playfulness, gentleness and strength. In the name of Christ, Amen."

Chapter 13

Reaffirmation of Marriage

It is generally recognized that a major turning point occurs after several years of marriage. When people marry, they inevitably marry images. They project onto the other what they want and need in a partner. The less mature they are, the less these projections will have any relation to reality.

They have some notion about what an ideal husband or wife ought to be like, and then choose as a partner someone with enough similarities to the image to arouse their interest. They also enter marriage with the notion that all of their personal problems will vanish, or at least that life will become much easier for them.

A third illusion of marriage is that intimacy will be easy.

After the honeymoon period of the marriage, it gradually becomes clear that none of these expectations is going to be fulfilled. Both partners have just as many problems as ever, their spouses are never going to live up to the partner's image of what they ought to be, and the moments of deep intimacy have been irregular. But instead of questioning their images of what things ought to be like, people usually tend to look around for someone to blame.

Some people blame themselves, saying that if only they could be different, then the partner would become the ideal spouse to which he or she is so richly entitled, and intimacy would come easily.

Others may blame their spouse, indicating that if only he or she would live up to the expected image, then intimacy would be easy and all problems would vanish. Others may occasionally blame in-laws, relatives, parents, neighbors, children, and so forth. But this is generally related to a more basic complaint about one's self or one's spouse.

A great deal of energy is then often expended in trying to force the spouse to live up to the image—to get him or her to change. It usually takes several years to realize that this is futile—there is no way to

doi:10.1300/5590_14

force the partner to change. The husband and wife are stuck with each other the way they are, and often experience a vague sense of uneasiness, defeat, bitterness, helplessness, and sometimes despair. This is a major impasse and calls for a significant and deliberate effort to transcend it. If successful, the couple will experience a new quality of love in their relationship and will come to love each other as persons rather than as images.

This rebirth of marriage deserves to be celebrated. The service that is presented here seeks to do that. It recognizes that people change and that relationships change. It is good for these changes to be creatively recognized and affirmed. It also expresses another issue: "Why do we stay married? Is it because we want to or because we have to?"

After several years of marriage, there are a lot of "have to" factors— children, furniture, finances, habit, a feeling that no one else would want me, or that my family couldn't get along without me, and so forth. If there is too much of the "have to," the partners will feel trapped. The remarriage ceremony may serve to bring to light some of the "want to" factors in the relationship and thus bring another bit of freedom.

I have used this service only once, at a "Reaffirmation Party." I have read parts of it to people in my office and have found it useful in this regard. It might also be used in connection with a wedding anniversary, a marriage enrichment workshop, or so forth.

PRINCIPLES OF REMARRIAGE

"Beloved friends, we are here tonight to celebrate with Mary and John as they affirm the new directions their lives together are taking. By our presence, we are saying to them, 'This is important. We are happy to be with you and to rejoice with you.'

"People enter marriage in many ways as children—caught up in the novelty and excitement of a new relationship, inspired by the promise of a new way of life.

"But along with the realistic expectations are certain images, romantic illusions. Each partner thinks that the two of them will instantly become an ideal husband or wife. They think that intimacy will be easy.

"But after several years of marriage, there comes the sobering realization that these dreams are not being totally fulfilled. Instead of finding that life has become easy, each spouse comes to understand his or her own unique responsibility for his or her existence and happiness.

"Instead of relying on the spouse changing, he or she comes to learn the more difficult and rewarding task of loving the spouse for what he or she is—for better and for worse.

"Instead of finding intimacy to be easy, he or she understands that conflict is inevitable and that intimacy is a pearl of great price, worth investing in, fighting for, and compromising for.

"A mature marriage then involves both togetherness and separateness, similarity and difference, conflict and forgiveness. It involves creating—deliberately creating occasions for intimacy, making the effort to love.

"A mature marriage involves freedom. And by your coming together on this day after a number of years of marriage, you are saying to each other and to your circle of friends and family, 'We are together because we choose to. Even if this legal tie did not exist, we would still choose to live together.'"

A CHARGE TO THE COUPLE

"Mary and John, I require and charge you both, as you stand in the presence of God, to understand anew your commitment to your relationship.

> It is better to be loving
> than to be right.
> It is better to be loved
> than to be approved.
> It is better to forgive
> than to get even.
> It is better to be forgiven
> than to be justified.
> It is better to be happy
> than to win."

Prayer

"Loving God, we are grateful for the gift of life, and for the gift of love that hungers within us, so that we reach out to touch and to be touched. Bless now these Thy children as they stand here this day.

May they be enabled to lay aside whatever guilt or bitterness may still be with them—for these only cling to the past. And wilt Thou awaken even more hunger within them, that they may find new ways of reaching out to each other and to the world. Grant them gentleness and courage and playfulness and love. In the name of Christ, Amen."

ACCEPTANCE OF RESPONSIBILITY

"Do you, John, now acknowledge Mary, whose hand you hold, to be your beloved wife, and do you unconditionally commit yourself anew to being her husband; to regard her as more important than any other, to become increasingly vulnerable to her, risking even more of what can be used against you; to renounce all forms of retaliation; to live with her and cherish her as long as you both shall live?"

"I do."

"Do you, Mary, now acknowledge John whose hand you hold, to be your beloved husband, and do you unconditionally commit yourself anew to being his wife; to regard him as more important than any other, to become increasingly vulnerable to him, risking even more of what can be used against you; to renounce all forms of retaliation; to live with him and cherish him as long as you both shall live?"

"I do."

To the guests:

"And will you, loved ones and friends, support Mary and John in this marriage, by helping create a world characterized by love and forgiveness? If so, say, 'I do.'"

"I do."

Prayer

"Loving God, we are grateful for the spirit of life that hungers within us and reaches out to other people. As John and Mary have reached out uniquely to each other, may they find tenderness and joy in touching and in being touched.

"As You have brought them together and sustained them, bless them anew, giving them a new vision of living. Enrich their lives through all the things they share together: times of boredom as well as times of joy and excitement; times of struggle and pain as well as times of love and peace. May they increasingly enjoy and love each other. In the name of Christ, Amen."

COMMENTS ON MARRIAGE

"John and Mary, you are as two trees that were transplanted so close to each other that their roots and branches became intertwined. Together they form one canopy to shade the earth, and to reach out to the warm sun and to protect the young trees that may grow beneath them.

"When leaves fall from the tree, they fertilize the earth. So with the experiences of life. When they are past, they feed our understanding and our ability to forgive.

"As the rain falls on the soil and the sun shines on the leaves and the wind blows in their branches, the trees will be sometimes competing and sometimes sharing, sometimes pushing against each other and sometimes supporting each other, sometimes fighting and sometimes loving. The places where they keep rubbing against each other will sometimes wear away the bark and become as an open wound, but will finally become a point of growing together, of engrafting. In being together and growing together, both trees inevitably influence each other—permanently. Each is now incomplete without the other.

"In a way this is sad. Many possibilities for your lives are now out of reach, dreams and fantasies about what you might have been and might have accomplished are no longer available to either of you. You have limited yourselves and each other, forever.

"But in many other ways, this is blessed, for your roots are now grounded in the solid earth of what is, rather than the vague unrealities of what might have been. And so your lives are real, and your love is real, and the affirmations you make are for that which is real."

EXCHANGE OF VOWS

"I love you, Mary, and with deep joy I take you again to be my beloved wife. I solemnly commit myself anew to being your husband, through all the dark times of life as well as the happy ones. I will do my best to bring to you playfulness, thoughtfulness, tenderness, generosity, and forgiveness, as long as we both shall live."

"I love you, John, and with deep joy I take you again to be my beloved husband . . ."

PRAYER OF AFFIRMATION

"Now, O Lord, bless these Thy people. Guide them into new areas of awareness and discovery and joy. Strengthen their commitment, enliven their play, soften their conflict, enrich their intimacy. In the name of Christ, Amen."

DECLARATION

"Now as your pastor, and as a spokesperson for each of you and for this new commitment to your relationship, I affirm that you, John and Mary, are anew husband and wife. What therefore God has blessed, let us acknowledge with gratitude and joy."

BENEDICTION

"Now may the Lord bless you and keep you . . ."

Chapter 14

Leaving Home

One of the important transitions of contemporary life is leaving home. In ancient times, children did not leave home in the same sense that they do today. Consequently, few leaving-home ceremonies have evolved over the years. Most of the "ceremonies" today are informal, such as a party with one's friends or a special meal with the family.

My friend and colleague Mary Callaway Logan developed a beautiful ceremony for her daughter. Hillary would be leaving for college soon and wanted to mark this important transition in a way that would acknowledge the world from which she came and point her to the world which she would be entering.

The setting would be a large deck on the back of a neighbor's home. Mary and Hillary designed a kind of maypole or canopy with twenty-two half-inch ribbons—one for each of the family, friends, and neighbors who would participate.

These ribbons were some ten feet long and reflected Hillary's favorite colors. These were tied together at one end through a small brass ring. This ring was eventually tied onto a tree limb that extended over the deck. A foot or so below that was a horizontal brass ring about a foot in diameter. Each ribbon was knotted once around this ring. A couple of feet below that was another horizontal brass ring about eighteen inches in diameter. Each ribbon was knotted around it also. This ring was about six feet above the ground. When Hillary stood in the center of the canopy, she was surrounded by ribbons. She told me later that she also felt surrounded by the love of the people present.

On the floor was a quiltlike cloth about five-feet square, onto which Mary and Hannah (Hillary's sister) had sewn a design full of symbolism for Hillary. The spiral was an important feature, as were symbolic references to water. This cloth lay on a slightly larger quilt her grand-

doi:10.1300/5590_15

mother had made. Standing on this meant symbolically that she was supported by the love and values of her grandmother.

⌒❧

The opening music was provided by a friend who played the harp and Hillary's sister who played the flute. Then her mother began reading.

MARY: This is a ceremony of blessing and sending forth of Hillary Grace Logan. We are gathered as your dear family, extended family, friends, the spirits of those who cannot be here, and the souls of your grandfathers. Each of us represents parts of your eighteen years among us.

KENT [Hillary's father]: We acknowledge the journey you are about to make, and want to send you forth with our blessings, signs of the abiding spirit, with solemnness and joy.

MARY: The journey outward is a journey to the center of your independent life. It is both a journey out, and a journey to the center. Nature is one teacher of the rhythm of this journey. Symbolized by the spiral, its line is never straight.

We listen to water, which always moves in a spiral, water which mediates heaven and earth in cloud form, which meanders in the river, whose flow reflects the moon. We look to fire, which burns in a spiral, which lives lovingly in the hearth, and which must be contained. We learn from the earth, that pours forth infinite variations of life as roots seek depth, and branches seek the sun. The air carries the breath of God's spirit to us, and in incense, carries prayers back to God.

One key to living into your future is to live the movement of Nature, bending, flowing, meandering, mediating, giving, receiving. This movement is a dance, infinitely creative.

JIM RULE [a family friend and Hillary's spiritual adviser]: The path to the center requires direction. Your soul's journey to realization of the One, its power, its nature, and its work, is yours alone to take. Along that way, each person here assented to help prepare you for that journey. Fate, calling, the Will of God brought us and you together. And so tonight we are here to celebrate the end of this stage of your preparation and the beginning of the next.

Look around you at the faces who have helped you build your way into the many worlds. We are grateful to have been called to be with you. We're grateful for your being, grateful for the opportunity you have given us to commit ourselves to a work of love, and grateful and proud to stand here with you.

This week, you leave for college. Hidden among the things you will haul with you are many unopened gifts. For you to look for them is useless, but given your determination and courage, at just the precise moment, under just the right circumstances, they will appear at hand. Then they will be yours to use. These are our going-away gifts—from those of us here you can see, and from the many hosts, powers, teachers, and helpers who also are present, whom you do not yet see.

As you ask, you will receive. I have that on the very best authority. So ask that your journey to the center of the One will continue and that our joy in you may be complete.

KENT: The path to the center requires reflection: When you look at your reflection in this mirror, seek first to see yourself through the eyes of God who loves you like a moonstruck love, who values you as a precious jewel. When Christ gave God's love flesh and passion, we learned that God eternally seeks us—shadows, blemishes, and all. The hope is that you may embrace your whole self in beauty. Look in the mirror and be all of who you are.

MARY: The path to the center requires love transformed. There have been many visible bonds of love: the daily nurture and protection of parents, grandparents, and sister; the guiding of spiritual companions; the extended family of "mothers and fathers"; your friends, schools, and travels.

[Hillary now stepped into the center of the canopy. Each participant took the end of a ribbon and formed a circle around the canopy.]

MARY: You will be cutting each of these visible bonds. Each cutting is an outward sign of the transformation of love from the visible to the invisible. Where they go is into the Mystery of the Spirits holding into the Unseen. As ties to the past are transformed, we will live the faith of the seed planted in fertile ground.

HILLARY: The words of Marianne Williamson [1996] seem especially appropriate for me tonight. "Our deepest fear is not that we are inadequate. Our deepest fear is that we are powerful beyond measure. It is our light, not our darkness, that most frightens us. We ask ourselves, Who am I to be brilliant, gorgeous, talented, fabulous? Actually, who are you *not* to be? You are a child of God. Your playing small doesn't serve the world. There's nothing enlightened about shrinking so that other people won't feel insecure around you. We were born to make manifest the glory of God that is within us. It's not just in some of us; it's in everyone. And as we let our own light shine, we unconsciously give other people permission to do the same. As we're liberated from our own fear, our presence automatically liberates others."

You have all given me this light, through your company, your guidance and your nurturing, your conversation and stories, your actions and teachings. These have nurtured my own light, which shines strong as I venture into these new waters of life. Thank you.

[Each participant now stepped toward Hillary and said something to her, perhaps with an embrace: what she has meant to him or her, what his or her dreams are for her, or so forth. He or she then lifted the ribbon toward Hillary, who cut it with scissors. The participant then placed the loose end of the ribbon around Hillary's shoulders. Mother and Father were last to do this.]

BENEDICTION: As we join hands in a circle, let us pray: "The Lord bless you and keep you . . ."

Music and refreshments followed.

⟨☙⟩

Hillary said this was a very important transition for her. The most important part was the cutting of the ribbons. She felt somewhat unworthy and sad, but also felt a deep sense of exhilaration and freedom.

Chapter 15

From Home to Nursing Home

INTRODUCTION

One of the fundamental realities of life is that change is difficult. Even when the change is a happy one, it carries with it a certain amount of distress. This is even more true of those changes that are unwanted and carry negative implications to those who are involved.

One of the most painful transitions that people face in the contemporary world is that of leaving one's home to enter a nursing home. One's home is often basic to one's sense of well-being. It is a refuge, a place to which to retreat, a familiar place in a chaotic and confusing world, a place associated with security and even nurture. It is a base in which one finds meaning and significance, and from which one enters into the activities of life. One has a certain sense of power in one's home; one can exert influence there that one can exert nowhere else. To lose one's home, for whatever reason, is to lose all of those deeper qualities and meanings.

This is not always true, of course. Many people have moved so often that they do not become attached to a place, to think of it as home. As people age, their attachments may be more tenuous. On the other hand, others may form attachments more quickly as they grow older. Memory may be a factor also. If one's memory is fading, the significance of home may be greater or less, depending on many factors. I think the safe approach is to assume that home is very important, regardless of the time one has lived there, and the amount of memory

This chapter is adapted: Copyright 1995 from "From Home to Nursing Home: A Ritual of Transition," by Henry Close, in *The American Journal of Family Therapy* 23(1). Reproduced by permission of Taylor & Francis, Inc., http://www.taylorandfrancis.com.

doi:10.1300/5590_16

loss one has suffered. Even people with severe memory loss often have moments of lucidity, indicating that the memories are still there, but are just unavailable most of the time.

When one enters a nursing home, it is because of losses. One can no longer care for oneself, even with help from others. With this physical and sometimes mental deterioration comes a loss of independence and even a loss of identity.

The ceremony that is offered here addresses the move from home to a nursing home. It presupposes a certain situation that is common but is certainly not universal: the home is one in which a husband and wife (let's call them Charles and Naomi) have raised their children. Charles is dead now, and Naomi has lived there alone for a few years. She is now unable to care for herself. The children (let's call them John and Robert) are unable to take her into either of their homes, so they finally persuade her to enter a nursing home.

The family has been fairly serious about their faith and active in a rather conservative religious community. The "home" addressed in this ceremony could be any home, and the person leaving could be any relative or even a friend, as could those who are addressed as children. The person who officiates should modify the ceremony appropriately to fit the realities of specific situations.

This ceremony as it is written is much too long. I wrote it that way deliberately to offer several options to the people who might use it. Feel free to pick and choose, to modify and adapt.

It is best for a ceremony to be officiated by someone who is not an integral part of the family circle, someone who has symbolic significance to the family, such as a minister, priest, rabbi, therapist, or doctor. Such an officiant speaks not only for one's family but also for one's broader community and for one's God.

When a parent must enter a nursing home, this changes the parent's relation to his or her children. Many adult children will welcome this transition as an opportunity to reciprocate, to become parental to the one who parented them. They are now able to give emotional and financial support, as an opportunity to live out their own maturity vis-à-vis their parent.

Other children may be greatly relieved that they are now no longer responsible for the day-to-day care of their parent. For still others, such a move can be quite traumatic. They may be indignant at the thought that Mother will no longer be there for them in the same way, to support and nurture and reassure. It is often true that Mother has been unable to do any of this for years, but as long as the structure of her life is unchanged, children can cling to the illusion that she is still able.

Many of the disagreements over dividing the furnishings—something that parents often see as incredibly insensitive—may stem from this anxiety. One of the functions of a ceremony such as this is to address these anxieties and to affirm people's loyalties to a higher reality.

In a typical situation, most of the furnishings will be divided among relatives and friends. This is often extremely difficult for the person leaving, because he or she often has a feeling of little or no control over the situation.

One way to gain a sense of control is to *give* away things rather than just abandon them. It would be impractical for every item to be given away, but perhaps one item could be given to each child—an item that had significance only to that child. These gifts could then symbolize the parent's continuing administration of his or her world. But if there is any question about sibling jealousy and rivalry, this should not be done.

If gifts are given, Mother might tell what this item meant to her and what she hopes it will mean to her child. If the children give gifts to the parent, make sure they are practical and not something to feel responsible for.

In many cultures, it is the custom for the aging parent to create a special blessing for each child and to bestow it at some auspicious occasion. In most of those traditions, it was clear that the primary blessing went to a specific child, usually the oldest son. To do that in our culture might incur the same sibling jealousies as the giving of gifts. The exception would be if there were only one child. Perhaps in that circumstance, this ceremony would be an appropriate occasion for such a blessing.

The blessing might have three parts: an appreciation of the child and his or her importance to the parent or family; an incident from childhood that is remembered with special warmth; and a wish for his or her future. Here is an example:

"I love you, John. By your life, you have taught me how to be a mother, and how to be a better human being—how to nurture and to forgive, and how to take a profound delight in another human being. I will never forget a time when you were five. Your father was sitting on the couch. When you walked into the room, you sensed how depressed he was, and walked over and kissed him warmly on the cheek. And my prayer for you is that your capacity to be tender, and to let people be tender to you, will grow and deepen and become an even more important part of your life."

It might also be appropriate for the child to write a blessing for the parent, and to bestow it at the same time.

It would be especially valuable if Naomi could take family (and friends) on a guided tour of the house, commenting on various pieces of furniture, pictures, and so forth—where and when she got them, and some of the memories associated with them. Others in the family could also comment. Then for the ceremony, everyone could sit around the dining room table with refreshments. Afterward, copies of the ceremony might be given to each family member.

OPENING PRAYER

"Eternal and loving God, You are the creator and sustainer of life and of all the things that make life worthwhile. You are the God of our yesterdays, our todays, and our tomorrows. And on this occasion, in which one chapter of life is brought to an end and another is to begin, we know that You are here too, to affirm, to sustain, to bless.

"This place, this home, is special to those gathered here. It is a sacred place, where sacred things have occurred: growth and healing, mistakes and forgiveness, laughter and tears, love and celebration. It is a place where meanings and attitudes and values have evolved. Untold thousands of memories are associated with this home, memories of the time and energy and love that helped convert it from a building into a home.

"There have been several homes in Naomi's life: the home of her birth and childhood in Seattle, the home of her teenage years in Mountain View, the home of her early marriage in Sacramento, the home here in which she has reared her children and enjoyed the maturing of her marriage, the home of her retirement, to which she will now move. Just as there are special memories associated with all these homes, so will there be special memories associated with her new home, memories of laughter, and challenge, and peace.

"We know that You are respectful of the difficulty of saying good-bye, the difficulty of change. We ask especially for Naomi and also for John and Robert, and for all who are involved in their lives, that they will know in the depths of their hearts that You love them, and take them seriously, and bless them. From this day forward, Amen."

THE MEANING OF HOME

"Beloved friends, we are here today to mark the closing of one chapter in Naomi's life and the beginning of another. As a transitional moment, this is an opportunity to reflect on the deeper meanings of her life and her home, and to celebrate those with her. A home is more than just a place; it is an inner quality of belonging, a sense of feeling at home in the world, of being at peace with one's self.

"After a hurricane destroyed one family's dwelling, a friend told the young boy he was very sorry they had lost their home. The boy said, 'Oh, we still have a home. We just don't have a place to put it.' And you, Naomi, still have a home, and you are relocating it to another place, just as you, John and Robert, still have an ancestral home, although it will now be located in your memories rather than externally.

"When this home and its many furnishings first passed into your hands, they were just things. But you have made them your own as you invested something of your spirit in them. You created the significance they had for you, and you will do so in the future with other places and other things and other events.

"Just as a book is more than paper and ink, or even than the words it contains, just as a piece of beautiful music is more than notes printed on a page, or sounds from the orchestra, so is home more than a building and its furnishings. Their essence consists of the feelings and meanings that resonate within your hearts and your minds."

SAYING GOOD-BYE

"It is now time to say good-bye to this place that has symbolized home for you. There may be many feelings involved: perhaps a sense of relief at not having to be responsible for a house that may be demanding more and more of your time; perhaps sadness at leaving that which is familiar; perhaps resentment at the things that have made this move necessary; perhaps fondness of the memories that will go with you.

"Many of the items in this home have a special significance. They are associated with special moments, special relationships, special memories, perhaps things that have been handed down from one generation to the next: maybe a chair in which your own mother rocked you as a child, and then became yours as you rocked your own children; maybe a picture that you and Charles purchased on a special trip that has been valued not only for its own sake, but also as a reminder of happy times.

"There may be things in the yard—a special tree that you planted or a bed of flowers—that are especially important to you. In your imagination, you can visit all these things, imagine yourself touching them lovingly, thanking them for the pleasures they have brought you, and then saying good-bye to them."

A LITURGY OF TRANSITION

LEADER: Blessed are You, O Lord, Who holds all the days of our lives in Your memory.

RESPONDENTS: We thank You, Lord, for the gift of life.

LEADER: Blessed are You, O Lord, Who in all circumstances gives purpose and direction to our lives.

RESPONDENTS: We thank You, Lord, for the gift of meaning.

LEADER: Blessed are You, O Lord, Who sees beneath the awkwardness of our efforts, to our deeper longings of the soul.

RESPONDENTS: We thank You, Lord, for the gift of forgiveness.

LEADER: Blessed are You, O Lord, Who walks with us through the dark places of life.

RESPONDENTS: We thank You, O Lord, for the gift of courage.

LEADER: Blessed are You, O Lord, Who cares about what happens.

RESPONDENTS: We thank You, O Lord, for the gift of love.

LEADER: Blessed are You, O Lord, Who holds our lives in Your hands.

RESPONDENTS: We thank You, O Lord, for the gift of peace.

ALL: Now and forevermore, Amen.

EXCHANGE OF GIFTS
AND BESTOWAL OF A BLESSING

This might be an appropriate place in the ceremony for the exchange of gifts, followed by the giving of blessing.

HYMN

It may be appropriate at this time to sing something, such as *one verse* of a familiar hymn, or a nursery song that has special meaning for the family. It might also be appropriate to have one or more family members read something, such as a familiar psalm (Psalm 23, for instance).

Prayer

"Now O God, we entrust to You the memories, the meanings, the qualities that are associated with this home and with the people who have lived here, to hold these memories in Your heart. We entrust to You the lives of these Your children: Naomi, in a new home that she will establish; John and Robert as they deal with the changes in their lives as a result.

"As new directions are taken, may they know that You go with them in each step of the way. May they feel Your stability in the midst of change, may they feel Your blessing, Your protection, Your presence. Forever and forever, Amen."

BENEDICTION

(If the parents have a favorite benediction, it should be used, especially one that addresses security in the midst of transition and change. The following is a familiar one and is often used in transitional ceremonies.)

"Now may the Lord bless you and keep you . . ."

Chapter 16

Funerals

When an elderly person dies after a long and debilitating illness, your mind and your heart may tell you different things. Your *mind* may tell you that this was inevitable, or that it was his or her time to go, or if there was much suffering, that it was for the best. But your *heart* says, "This was Mamma; this was Daddy," or in the heart-wrenching tragedy of Terri Schiavo, "This was my little girl." Nothing the *mind* can say can negate that anguish. Only a language of the heart, such as a ceremony, can address that loss.

Probably all cultures and spiritual traditions have ceremonial ways of dealing with death. In this chapter, I want to suggest a few principles and comments that might be utilized along with the rites of the family's own religious tradition. This is from a hypothetical service for a widow (Louise) who died after a long illness, leaving behind two children and four grandchildren.

"There are many transitions in life; all of them impact a family forcibly—especially transitions that involve the death of a loved one. With the death of Louise, there is the ending of one generation and a transition to the next. Karen and Jeff are now the senior generation, with Will, Ben, Kelly, and Wanda becoming the middle generation, with the first of a new generation yet to be born. There is a sense that we not only move through life, but life moves through us, and we pass on our values, our faith, our love as we move from one generation and into another. Every generation has its own responsibilities, its own wisdom, its own priorities, its own satisfactions.

Some of the material in this chapter was adapted from my article "Metaphor in Pastoral Care," *The Journal of Pastoral Care and Counseling,* December 1984, and is used with the publisher's permission.

"When a loved one dies, especially one who is the culmination of her generation, it underscores some of the difficult realities of life, some of the realities of our own finiteness. Some years ago, when my own mother died, I jotted down some reflections. As I have reread these in the past few days, they have seemed to express some themes that are universal, and I wanted to read them with you today.

"'There is a quality of incompleteness about every intimate relationship. No two people really touch each other to the extent that their relationship calls for. Our ties with any loved one call for a depth of contact that never happens fully. Even in our deepest moments of sharing, there is inevitably some obstacle, some reserve, some holding back that thwarts the intimacy we intend and for which we hunger. This is simply the way it is for us as human beings. We are imperfect, and our relationships are imperfect.

"'We are made acutely aware of this incompleteness when a loved one dies. There is inevitably some sense of guilt and resentment over the incompleteness. We think of things we should have said, but did not; things we should have done, but did not; feelings and experiences we should have shared, but did not. We think of things he or she should have said and done and shared, but did not. No doubt there is some reality to all the things we regret. But even if we had done everything we knew to do, the incompleteness would still have been there, because we are all human. So the forgiveness we owe ourselves and our loved one is not only for things that actually could have been different, but also for the imperfections that permeate our whole existence as human beings.'

"If I were to continue, I think I would put it in the form of a letter, addressed to my mother. 'As I think of your death and how I will remember you, I am aware of two realities. When I think of the happy times, the positive things about the ways you were a parent to me, I tend to idealize you, to put you on a pedestal. For one thing, I think you would like that. That is the way I would like my children to remember me.

"'On the other hand, when I think of unhappy times, the negative things about the way you were a parent to me, I tend to devalue you. The reality is that you were just an ordinary human being with strengths and weaknesses, assets and liabilities, and your way of being a parent grew out of all these factors, just like your parents were with you, and just like I am with my children.

"'One thing, though, was consistent. I always knew that you loved me—not always wisely, but always truly. Sometimes your love was mixed with demands, sometimes with possessiveness, sometimes with irritability, but underneath everything I knew that you really loved me just for me—whether I was obedient or successful or whatever. I knew that basically you had my best interest at heart, more so than any other human being I would ever encounter.

"'Now that I have children of my own, I can understand all these things, and remember you with warmth and love, with appreciation for who you were, and forgiveness for what you were not.'

"And now we remember you, Louise, with warmth and tenderness, with understanding and forgiveness, and most of all, with appreciation."

⹋

Many years ago, I conducted two funerals involving very disturbed and painful family relationships.

In the first family, the surviving husband described his marriage as "twenty-six years of hell," although he obviously had many tender feelings toward his deceased wife as well. In the second family, the surviving wife had recently—with much reluctance—filed for divorce after struggling with her husband's drinking and abusiveness for over twenty years.

I was asked to do the funerals because I had been marginally involved with them, and I was the only minister they knew. I saw these people only once before the funeral and once afterward. So there would be no opportunity for a normal pastoral ministry over an extended period of time. The funeral service itself would therefore have to carry the major part of the pastoral ministry. But the intense ambivalences made this a difficult task.

If I addressed only the positive aspects of the relationships, I would fulfill only a part of their need. I would help them honor the deceased family member and would contribute to his or her being respectfully remembered by other family and friends who attended the services. But this would leave the negative feelings of guilt and resentment unacknowledged; it would make these feelings more difficult to deal with in the days ahead. Because these painful feelings would probably be the most difficult ones for the family to deal with, for me to say nothing about this dimension of their grieving would have been grossly irresponsible.

On the other hand, however, if I acknowledged the negative side of the relationships, no matter how gently and lovingly I spoke, I would most surely embarrass the family by making public their difficulties. I would expose the family to what they would think would be negative judgments by their families and friends. My comments might address an inner need, but the value of this would be negated by the inevitable social embarrassment.

It finally occurred to me that I could resolve this dilemma by modifying the reflections I had written at the time of my mother's death and reading them at the funeral service. I would introduce them by saying that I wanted to share with them some of my thoughts that I had written when my mother died some years ago. (Some might take issue with the "dishonesty" of revising my comments and then reading them as though they had been written years earlier, but I felt this was emotionally honest even though it was factually false. What was important was what I said, not the details of how I came to say it.)

The fact that I wrote them in the past about someone else—my own mother, no less—would immediately soften anything that sounded harsh or negative. It would put my comments in the framework of life itself rather than the framework of their particular families and difficulties. It would be a statement of *my* participation in the universal human dilemma. They could take from that whatever personal meanings and applications they chose.

My impression after the first service was that my predictions had been accurate. I had said what needed to be said and had not embarrassed anyone in the process. After the first service, the husband said the service was "very beautiful and very personal."

I felt that something a bit different needed to be said at the second service, so I revised my comments again for that occasion and then read them in the same way. In this situation, too, I felt that I had ministered sensitively to a very disturbed family. A close friend of the family told me that she knew that the husband had had many ups and downs, and that my comments seemed right to the point. The son asked me for a copy that he might read at a memorial service in his father's home town, saying that my comments really put his mind at rest.

It was a written way of addressing difficult situations in order to bypass possible resistances and embarrassments.

Another funeral service was for a woman who had never married but who was a very attentive and loving second mother for her nieces and nephews. These are some of my comments.

"In a normal family, a child is conceived and carried and birthed in love. The love is not for his or her personality but for something much deeper, for his or her soul, his or her being. Then many layers of living and meaning are added to that: independence, learning how to get along with other people, various forms of competence, contributions, and status, mistakes and achievements, successes and failures, embarrassments and satisfactions. As one approaches the final days of life, these layers are progressively stripped away—the successes and failures (both impostors, according to Kipling) lose their importance. Embarrassments and satisfactions are forgotten. Mistakes and successes fade away. What is left is what is most basic—being surrounded by love. That is what is really important, and we bring now our love and appreciation for Aunt Mary."

Chapter 17

A Ceremony for Grieving

Several people in our congregation had suffered serious loss during the previous year. A teenage boy committed suicide; a dearly loved grandfather died slowly of cancer; two couples divorced; a man was crippled in an accident. As the minister of counseling, I felt these situations called for something more than one-on-one pastoral care, so I designed the service I am describing here. If this ceremony were held in a non-Christian setting, such as a synagogue, the references to Christ would of course be omitted.

Two weeks before and also one week before the ceremony (which was to be held, appropriately, on All Saints' Day), I put an announcement in the church newsletter and an insert in the bulletin.

> A Ceremony for Grieving: Many people in our communities have suffered painful losses that are slow to heal: the loss of a loved one, a miscarriage, the end of a relationship, the loss of health and independence. It is often difficult to grieve adequately so that one can move on with one's life.
>
> There are many steps that need to be taken. One such step might be a formal ceremony for those who are grieving. This service will be offered on Monday, November 1, at 7:00 in the sanctuary of the church. Everyone is invited: those who are still grieving a loss of some kind, and those of you who by your presence wish to support your friends in their healing.

This chapter is based on my article "A Ceremony for Grieving," *The Journal of Pastoral Care and Counseling,* Spring 2002, used with the publisher's permission. Some of the material (story of fire victims) was adapted from my book *Metaphor in Psychotherapy,* and is used with the publisher's permission.

doi:10.1300/5590_18

Many people have found it helpful to write a kind of "letter" addressed to the one whose loss you feel so intensely. In the letter, include a section in which you tell the person that you forgive him or her for all the ways he or she has hurt you, and ask for his or her forgiveness for the ways you have hurt him or her. These letters—which of course are optional—will be collected during the service and burned. The ashes will then be buried respectfully in a box in the church cemetery.

On the Sunday before the ceremony, I announced it from the pulpit. I summarized the announcement that was in the bulletin and added, "When I first ran across the idea of writing letters to a deceased loved one, it sounded kind of hokey to me. But I wrote letters to both my parents and found it very meaningful. It brought back memories I hadn't thought of in years."

The afternoon of the service, I dug a hole about a foot deep in the cemetery and put some large sticks around it, so no one would step into it. That evening, I brought to the church a small wooden box, a shovel, two flashlights, a large aluminum mixing bowl and a grate to facilitate burning, matches, lamp oil, a potholder, a spatula, a spray bottle filled with water, and a fire extinguisher.

There was an insert in the bulletin for people who had not already done so to write something to the deceased loved one. I then repeated the newsletter announcement:

A CEREMONY FOR GRIEVING
Blessed are those who mourn,
for they shall be comforted.

The back of the bulletin was not needed for the service, so I used this space for the following:

> I come to your grave.
> Memories, forgotten feelings, tears,
> Stir within my heart.

The following poem was written by Friedrich Ruckert, on the death of his young daughter.

When your dear mother comes through the door,
   and I turn my head toward her,
   my glance falls first not on her face,
   but on the place lower on the doorframe
   where your dear little face would be,
   if you had come into the room with her, bright-eyed,
   as you used to do my daughter.
When your dear mother comes into the room,
   in shimmering candlelight,
   it is for me still as though you come into the room
   with her,
   slipping behind her, as you used to do my daughter.*

Grieving is like the healing of a wound. At first, there is a time of quiescence for the cells along the edge of the cut to recover from the trauma. Then the cells begin to reach out across the chasm. As they reach, they fill in the places that have been injured. Finally they make contact with those cells on the other side of the wound, interlace with them, and we say the wound has healed.

The bulletin included the following material.

INTRODUCTION

Final good-byes are never easy. In addition to the pain of loss, there is inevitably a sense of incompleteness in our good-byes. This service seeks to address that aspect of the grieving process. Sometimes it helps to put one's thoughts and feelings in writing. If you have not already written something to your loved one, you will find a blank piece of paper in the bulletin for that purpose. If you do not wish to write something, please just fold the paper and bring it forward later in the service. You may wish simply to let the words take form in your imagination.

The newsletter announcement was then summarized.

---

*I have tried without success to find the translator of this poem, so that appropriate credit can be given.

A PRAYER OF CONFESSION

[I introduced this prayer by saying that the word "confession" had several references. There is a confession of sin; there is also a confession of faith. This prayer is a confession of neediness.]

Eternal and loving God, we bring to You the inmost concerns of our hearts, knowing that You walk patiently with us through the dark shadows of our lives. We have all suffered losses that are often deeply painful:

the death of a loved one;
the death of a relationship;
the death of dreams and hopes.

We confess to You how difficult it is to grieve.

So we entrust to You
words that have been difficult to say,
feelings that have been difficult to express,
good-byes that need to be said.

As You walk with us in our grieving,
walk also with us into the newness of life.

LEADER: We are assured that God hears our prayers and sustains us in our grief. In Jesus Christ, we are supported and nurtured and loved.
PEOPLE: Thanks be to God.

LITANY

LEADER: Loving God, You have come into the darkness of our world that we may feel your presence even in our despair.
PEOPLE: Lord, hear the prayers of our neediness.
LEADER: You have come to walk with us through the valleys of the shadow of death.
PEOPLE: Lord, hear the prayers of our weakness.

LEADER: You have come to lift up those who have fallen, and to sustain those who suffer.

PEOPLE: Lord, hear the prayers of our pain.

LEADER: You have come to comfort those who are afflicted.

PEOPLE: Lord, hear the prayers of our grief.

LEADER: You have come to sustain us when our tomorrows seem bleak and empty.

PEOPLE: Lord, hear the prayers of our fear.

LEADER: You have come to bring strength and courage to face the tomorrows of our lives.

PEOPLE: Lord, hear the prayers of our hope.

LEADER: You come to lead us into the light of renewal and life.

PEOPLE: Lord, hear the prayers of our hearts.

.⌒⌒⌒)

For the opening prayer, I prayed: "In the quietness of this moment, we would open our hearts to You, O God, who sees beneath the veneers of our daily living, and touches the depths of our lives. For some of us here, there is still much pain in those deep places of our lives. For some, it is a sharp, stabbing pain. For others, it is a dull, heavy ache. Sometimes it takes hold of our consciousness, so that we can attend to nothing else. Sometimes it recedes into the background. But we always know it is there. We know we must face it.

"Let us know, O God, that we do not face it alone, that You are always with us, that we always live in Your thoughts and in Your caring. Help us to forgive those who have hurt us by what they have done, and for what they have not done—especially those who are no longer living. Help us to forgive ourselves for what we have done and for what we have not done—for You forgive us. And lead us through the darkness and into the light of a new day. In the name of Christ, Amen."

MEDITATION

For the meditation, I wanted first to establish rapport, so I told about people who had experienced terrible losses. I then wanted to offer some perspectives for healing and growth, so I talked about how certain people had dealt with the pain of bereavement.

"Some years ago, I knew a woman whose daughter and four grandchildren had died in a fire. She was so distraught the family wouldn't let her grieve—they wouldn't let her go through the painful process of saying good-bye. They wouldn't let her go to the funeral. They hid all the pictures. They wouldn't even let her talk about her anguish. Very quickly, she was so disturbed that she was admitted to the psychiatric unit at the county hospital, and then to the Georgia Mental Health Institute, where I was chaplain. The time she was there was a time for grieving—painful, anguished grieving. But after a few weeks, she was ready to be discharged.

"When she left, she said that the process of healing had been like being in a barren room with a huge piece of ice blocking the door. She would rub on the ice, to try to melt it away, but very quickly her hands would become so cold she would have to back off and rub them together to try to get them warm. Then she would rub the ice some more, and would again have to back off. But finally she had melted a hole in the ice big enough for her to crawl out of.

"I think most grieving is like that, at least to some extent. Our world becomes smaller, barren, colder, with a sense of being trapped with no way out.

"One woman's husband had been killed senselessly by a drunk driver just days after she had told him she was pregnant with their first child. Her friends' advice was well-meant but confusing. One friend told her that she needed to put this out of her mind. What had happened had happened. No amount of grieving would bring back her husband, and she needed to devote her time and energy to preparing for the birth of her child.

"She knew there was some validity to this advice. She did need to get on with her life. But pretending it wasn't there wouldn't make the block of ice go away.

"Another friend told her the exact opposite, saying that dealing with this tragedy needed to be her number one priority. She needed to put everything else in her life on hold until she had faced this tragedy and dealt with it.

"The woman knew there was a grain of truth in this. She knew she needed to grieve. But she just could not bear to face the full intensity of that loss for more than a few minutes at a time. It was like her friend was trying to hold her hands against the ice continually, and that wasn't possible.

"Unfortunately, no one else can rub the ice for you, to help it melt away. No one else has access to it. Even God can't make it just go away. What your loved ones and your friends can do, what God does, it to help you to get your hands warm, for the time when you must rub the ice again. They can hold your hands lovingly next to their hearts to help them to get warm.

"Tonight, here, we are with people who support us and love us, people who hold our hands lovingly next to their hearts.

"There are different kinds of grief. A friend's wife died slowly of cancer. They spent much time together in those final months reminiscing on their lives, celebrating their lives. Every night, my friend would sit at the foot of the bed and rub her feet while they talked, saying their good-byes to each other.

"Another friend said that as long as her mother was clinging to life, there was always something she could do for her—bring her flowers, stroke her arm, talk lovingly to her about memories of childhood. But when she died that was no longer possible, and there was a deep sense of helplessness relative to her mother. She had to move her, in her mind, from being one whom she nurtured and for whom she prayed, to one of that group of people for whom she was grateful. She felt the loss especially keenly when she saw flowers for sale and realized there was now no way to bring them to her mother.

"My parents both died in nursing homes. Most of my grieving was during the months they were there, and I watched them gradually lose their hold on life. Afterward, there were only a few occasions when I felt a deep sense of sadness—like when my oldest daughter got married. Mother would have loved being there.

"But not all grieving is in that context. A friend's infant child died of a sudden illness. He said that one of the hardest things about this was that it was a violation of the natural order of things. How can such a thing be? You expect your parents to die. There is a fifty/fifty chance that your spouse will die before you—hopefully, in the fullness of time. But not your child. It's just not right. So in addition to his grief for the loss of a child, he had to come to grips with a world that was not reliable, where things did not always happen as they were supposed to.

"Even more painful is the death of a rebellious child—the prodigal son, like King David's son Absolom. One father said he knew that deep down, beneath all the destructiveness, all the debris of life, his son loved his family and would some day get his act together. He was even showing signs of, as the father put it, 'coming to himself.' But he died while driving under the influence of drugs. It finalized his life at the point of his rebellion, at the point of his pathology.

"But the father knew that his son had encountered God. He had experienced whatever judgment was appropriate. He had experienced God's forgiveness and healing. He knew that if his son could come back, he would affirm his love for his family. He would ask them to forgive him for the pain he had caused them. He would tell them he forgave them for the ways they had hurt him. And from that perspective, the family could begin the process of grieving.

"One woman's beloved daughter was murdered in the sabotage of the Pan Am airliner over Lockerbee, Scotland. 'My only child is dead,' she writes, 'and for me grief is constant and permanent. . . . I get up every day, go places, meet people. I live my diminished life. But grief is always there. I am in pain all the time. Theo wanted to be an actress and singer. We shared a love of music. We shared a love of plays. Music is gone from my life now, and I can't walk into a theater. I go out of my way not to have to pass one. Call it living defensively, this always being prepared for the unexpected reminder, always being on guard against the shock that creates panic, this eternal vigilance against the innocent remark that will bring on depression . . .' (*Time*, July 26, 1996).

"It doesn't have to be this way. One man was in this kind of despair for a long time after his wife had been murdered. In a strange kind of way, he felt it would be unfaithful to her for him to laugh, or to enjoy a symphony, or eventually to love someone else.

"One night it was like his wife came to him, and he could hear her voice: 'I want your life to be richer for what we shared, rather than poorer for what we no longer share.

"I have often thought of how a tree survives the harshness of winter, when the days become short, so there is more darkness than light, and the world becomes cold and foreboding. In response to the darkness and coldness of the world, the life of the tree, the sap, withdraws from the world and seeks the safety and warmth of roots that are buried deep in the earth.

"During the harshness of winter, nothing is asked of the tree but to survive. The leaves fall off and the tree becomes barren and ugly.

"But beauty is not called for in the winter. All that is called for is survival. There may be ice storms that break some of the limbs of the tree, leaving an open wound. But healing is not called for in winter. To all outward appearances, the tree is lifeless and dead. But growth is not called for in winter. All that is asked of the tree is to survive.

"Finally in the beginning of spring, the days become longer, and there is more light than darkness. The harshness and cold of winter give way to the warmth of spring. In response to this light and warmth, the tree comes to life again. The sap is drawn by the increasing warmth of the world up through the trunk and out into the limbs and branches and twigs. Only then are healing and growth asked of the tree. But during the coldness and harshness of winter, all that is asked is to survive.

"Grieving is like that in some ways. We are caught up in the winter of our losses. We despair of spring ever coming. But down in the deepest grounding of our lives, to which we withdraw, there, surrounding us with warmth and protection, is God. And spring does come, in its own time, and we can feel alive again.

"Friends often try to comfort us, by telling us the loved one is with God and is at peace. That's true, but that usually does not assuage the sense of loss that we feel so acutely. My loved one is not here with me. And that's what I grieve.

"One man, following the death of his parents, visited the home in which he had been raised—which was still in the family. He went from room to room, touching the walls and furniture, like people coming to the wall of the Vietnam Veterans Memorial to touch the name of a loved one. All kinds of memories flooded his mind, memories that were now entrusted to God. With each memory—even the painful ones— he breathed a prayer of gratitude: 'Thank you for these thousands of pebbles that have been part of the foundation of my life.'"

"Where is God when we suffer so deeply? Where is God in our pain? The answer is that God is here, with us, in the midst of our struggling. The Word became flesh, and dwelt among us. The Word became flesh, and suffered with us. The cross shouts to us that God is here, in the darkness, with us. The psalmist does not say that God lifts us out of the valleys of the shadow of death, but that God walks with us through those valleys. Deeper than our grief, deeper than our hopelessness and anguish, deeper even than our doubts, there we experience God."

I then prayed the pastoral prayer:

"Now O Lord, we thank You for the safe places to which we can retreat during the winters of our lives, for You are there to protect and to sustain us. We thank You for the springtimes that call us to life again, for You are there also, to encourage and bless us. We thank You for the people who have contributed to our lives, and have meant so much to us that we are devastated at their loss. And so we commit to You the deepest yearnings of our hearts, in the name of Christ our Lord, who taught us to pray together, . . . [the Lord's Prayer.]"

I then invited people to bring their letters to the front, where I stood holding the aluminum bowl with the grate inside. I asked them to speak the name of the person (or situation) to whom the letter was addressed, using the name they used in the letter ("Daddy," for instance, rather than "Father"). I put in my letters at that time.

Every person brought something to place in the bowl. Most brought a single sheet of folded paper. One person brought three envelopes, each containing a letter to a different loved one. Another person had three letters rolled into small scrolls and tied with ribbons.

We then went to the church cemetery, poured lamp oil into the bowl, and burned the letters. I asked the people to use this time to remember memories of their loved ones and to commit these memories to God as their letters burned. We then prayed the Lord's Prayer together.

Even with a grate, it can take a long time for paper in a bowl to burn. So after a minute or so, I sprayed water into the bowl to extinguish the remnants of the fire, used the potholder to pick it up, and used the spatula to scrape the ashes into a small wooden box. The box was placed into the ground, and I invited everyone to shovel in a bit of dirt. I then said the benediction.

Social worker Dorothy Miller does a somewhat similar ceremony on November 1 (All Saints' Day) in her church garden. Each person brings a small picture (or object that belonged to the person) and says a few words about the loved one. There are then prayers and a song before going inside for refreshments (personal communication).

The weather on the night of the service was miserable, and I did not know whether anyone other than my wife would come to this service. I expected maybe three or four persons. To my surprise, there were about twenty-five people—almost 10 percent of the church's membership! Many tears were shed, many people were hugging each other, and many people told me this had been a very meaningful service for them.

Chapter 18

Creating Other Ceremonies

There are many other occasions in life in which a formal ceremony might be appropriate. Some of these might be conducted in a place of worship or the privacy of the pastor's or therapist's office. Some might be held in a hospital room; others might involve family and/or friends at a party.

At least three things should be addressed in a ceremony: a recognition of loss and the change of identity that is implied by the loss, one's new status in the community, and a new commitment to the future.

Often a sense of guilt or shame maybe related to the situations a ceremony addresses. These can be addressed explicitly or implicitly through words that convey acceptance and forgiveness.

The officiant is someone who represents the community of which the person is a part. This is usually a clergyperson.

A typical ceremony (which doesn't have to be very long) has several parts. First there is the introduction, which may be in the form of a prayer. "Why are we here?"

Then there is a description of the situation, recognizing that which is being left behind and the ambivalence of change, and accepting the responsibilities of the new future. These may then be followed by an allegory or parable.

In a meditation or prayer, I want first to talk about how painful the situation is that is being addressed. This is to establish rapport. If people believe I really understand their pain, they are more likely to take me seriously when I talk about hope. Refer to the prayers and the meditation in the Ceremony for Grieving for examples of this principle.

A litany will be appropriate in many ceremonies. This is a kind of responsive prayer. The officiant reads a sentence describing some aspect of the situation, and the people read a response.

doi:10.1300/5590_19

There is often a statement from the person(s) addressed in the ceremony. This might be an exchange of vows, as in a wedding. Or a bereaved person may read a letter to the loved one who has died.

The ceremony may involve something tangible and an activity connected with it: food to be shared, candles that are lit, water with which to wash one's hands, something to be buried.

There are usually readings of some kind—scripture, allegory, or poetry.

Finally the leader affirms the new future the participants now enter. The ceremony then ends with a final prayer and benediction.

TURNING OFF THE LIFE-SUPPORT SYSTEM

Many families are faced with the incredibly difficult choice of whether to turn off the life-support system. In a hypothetical situation, Thomas had made a living will. If there is no chance that he will recover, he does not want his life prolonged by artificial means. Or as he put it, he does not want the process of dying prolonged artificially.

He had read of a woman with serious brain damage. The oldest son lived in the same city and saw her every day. One day she suffered a serious setback from which there was no chance of recovery. The doctors told him they could withhold treatment and she would die within a day or so, but they would need his permission to do this.

The son was quite willing; he felt Mother would not want to be kept alive artificially. But he also felt the need to consult with his siblings. The doctors told him they needed to make a decision immediately. He was unable to contact the siblings, and so told the doctors to keep his mother alive.

She "lived" for another several weeks. Frequent spasms would wrack her body. The son had been told that she could feel no pain, but he was not convinced. He wept practically every time he saw her and deeply regretted not allowing treatment to be discontinued. The siblings too regretted that he had not taken this step.

Thomas was irate at the thought that such a thing might happen to him. In his living will, he forbade his family, his insurance company, or Medicare from paying one cent to the hospital or to the physicians to prolong his "life" in that manner.

Thomas suffered a severe stroke a few weeks later. At first, there was hope. But after a second stroke, it was clear that he would never regain consciousness. After much consultation with his physician and the minister of their church, the family decided to discontinue treatment—to turn off the life-support system.

But they wanted to do this as a family, respectfully, with an appropriate ceremony, rather than delegate it to the medical staff, which would have seemed cold and impersonal.

Prior to the ceremony, each family member spent time with Thomas alone. They were asked to say to him whatever they needed to say, as though he could hear and understand. If there were unresolved issues, let these be addressed respectfully. It could also be a time for expressing regrets and for appreciation.

Each family member would also be asked to say a short good-bye to Thomas during the ceremony.

Each person present would then take the cord to the life-support system and pull it from the wall together.

APPROACHING DEATH

An increasing number of people who are terminally ill are aware of their impending death. Many of them would like to have some kind of gathering with family (and friends) to reminisce and to say good-bye. If this takes the form of a ceremony, it should be in the form of a celebration. It might include an opening prayer, opportunities for guests to tell about incidents they remember about the person, and to say something personal to him or her. There would be similar opportunities for the dying person. A prayer may then be followed by refreshments.

PHYSICAL LOSS

Many people suffer significant losses due to illness or accident. To be confined to bed or to the use of a walker is a serious loss of independence. So is the loss of hearing or sight. Losses such as these also bring a loss of self-esteem—especially for men. Much of our sense of well-being is based on our being able to accomplish things. When that is compromised, we suffer emotionally and spiritually. It may feel like our body has become our enemy.

Many people feel a sense of shame when their bodies will no longer function as they wish them to. I know this sounds irrational, but it is nevertheless true. At some level, we feel that if we can no longer function optimally, we will no longer be accepted as a full member of our community.

We also suffer when the losses are due to advancing years. The older we get, the higher the "price" we must pay to stay alive. With the loss of mobility there is often a loss of contact with friends and loved ones. They must now come to us, rather than our being able to go to them. Many friends hesitate to visit because they don't know what to say.

A ceremony would acknowledge these realities, and emphasize acceptance and forgiveness. We need to forgive our bodies for betraying us. A ceremony would also address friends and loved ones, affirming their ties and their responsibilities. A ceremony might also affirm the broader communities to which the person belongs—church, social groups, and so forth.

MATERIAL LOSS

A serious material loss, such as a home destroyed by fire or flood, often leaves one with a pervading sense of helplessness. If one's belongings are damaged, it is easy to feel that one's connectedness with the community is also damaged.

A ceremony might focus on one's ties with the community and the support of friends and neighbors.

JOB LOSS

A similar situation occurs when one has lost one's job. This too is often accompanied by feelings of shame and helplessness: "Maybe if I had done more, I might not have been laid off!"

In our culture, a man's (and to some extent a woman's) identity is closely related to his work. When the work is gone, a man may feel adrift, directionless, abandoned. No one likes feeling unnecessary, or feeling that he was expendable and someone else was not.

For many people, work has been like a second family. The people he sees every day become important to him. They are part of his network of connectedness with the family of humanity. Now this is gone.

It is awkward for him now to be around his friends, because they don't know what to say. Their words of encouragement are often shallow and unrealistic. Or they may simply avoid him.

Financial concerns are important. What looked like a secure future is now compromised. To find a new job, he needs energy and initiative. But the emotional impact of losing one's job tends to erode away energy and initiative.

ORGAN TRANSPLANT

Organ transplants are becoming more and more common. With the enormous complexities of the medical procedures, it is easy to lose sight of the emotional and spiritual issues that may be involved. Your own body has lost its integrity, and you are alive only because of someone else's body. You have suffered the loss of your health, and you are alive because someone else has lost his or her life.

There is often an uneasy sense of guilt. Maybe this heart (or other organ) could have gone to someone who deserved it more than I did. Maybe the money it took could have been better spent for other worthwhile purposes.

At first, this organ is an alien, emotionally as well as physically. The reaction of the body as well as the psyche is to reject that which is alien. There are drugs to help the body accept it, but there is usually little emotional support to help the psyche incorporate this organ into one's image of self.

No matter how irrational these concerns may be, they are nonetheless real and can be very destructive.

A ceremony might take place at a party. It could address the issues I have mentioned and then use the symbol of adoption. People usually adopt when they cannot conceive—when their own bodies do not function as they would like. Adoptions are expensive.

In an adoption, you take into your family and into your heart that which once was strange, alien. As you incorporate this child, you soon learn to love him or her, to regard him or her as your very own. This is the goal of the organ recipient as well.

The ceremony might then ask for your commitment to follow the principles of good health: exercise, diet, medication, checkups, and a life as free from stress as possible. These are a small price to pay for staying alive. It would encourage your commitment to saying no to health-endangering actions, and to too many responsibilities. It would ask for your commitment to things that make your life interesting and worthwhile: activities, time with loved ones and friends, hobbies, spiritual centeredness, and so forth.

Finally, the ceremony would ask for commitments from loved ones and friends to maintain their ties with you, so that you are lovingly included in their lives and the community they represent.

MISCARRIAGE

The emotional impact of a miscarriage is often hard for an outsider to understand. The child who has been lost was never seen by anyone else. The woman is not expected to grieve very much, so there is often little more than a perfunctory expression of condolences. After a few days, people stop being solicitous. Or they may dismiss the loss by telling her that she can always have another baby. (When people feel they *must* say something, they often say something stupid.)

Other people may have told her that a miscarriage is nature's way of disposing of an imperfect child. However true this may be, it is not what the woman needs to hear. She needs to hear that her loss and her shame are taken seriously by those whose love and support she needs.

The woman usually feels a vague sense of shame that her body is imperfect. Or she may blame herself for the miscarriage—she exercised too much, she ate inappropriately, or something else. Many times, there may be a germ of truth to this. Maybe the mother was not careful enough with her physical health. In that case, she needs forgiveness as well as affirmation.

One woman was absolutely certain that her baby was going to be a boy. She had already bought boy's clothes, painted the room a pale blue, and picked out a boy's name. When an ultrasound examination revealed that it was female, she was terribly distraught. As far as she was concerned, the boy had died. The fact that she was going to have a girl did not soften the loss of the boy. When she lost the fetus, she felt her distress may have caused the miscarriage.

A ceremony to address losses such as these might be held as a regular funeral, or in a pastor's office, with a few friends and family present. The woman might want to write a letter to the baby who has died and read it at the ceremony. It would then be disposed of respectfully. An important part of the ceremony might be the naming of the baby, and perhaps lighting a candle in memory of the child. If the mother wants the baby baptized, the pastor should find some way to do this symbolically. (I understand that Sister Jane Marie Lamb's book *Bittersweet . . . Hellogoodbye* [1989], is a collection of suggested pregnancy loss rituals and prayers. Unfortunately, I have not yet found a copy of this book.)

POSTPARTUM DEPRESSION

The birth of a child marks many changes in a woman's life, both in relation to herself and in relation to her community. While pregnant, there was a growing level of activity in her womb, as the baby became more and more animated. Now that is gone, and her body is suddenly quiet and empty, her womb has been abandoned. A sense of sadness and emptiness may be overwhelming. While she was pregnant she was probably the center of attention, but now must share that attention with the newcomer.

A ceremony in this situation would need also to be a celebration. It would need to be highly specific, for every woman's situation is different. It might include the baby's father, for there are many changes in his life also. The ceremony might include a prayer, a litany, a meditation, and/or an allegory. In it, the parents might talk of their dreams and wishes for the child as he or she becomes part of the family life they share together. Refreshments would also be important, as eating has many implications related to bonding and nurturing.*

AFTER A FUNERAL

In some traditions, there is a ceremony a year after the death of a loved one. The year is regarded as a necessary time of grieving, of

---

*The Web site aplacetoremember.com has several books related to miscarriage and infant death.

adapting to the loss. Ideally, other loved ones take on some of the responsibilities of the bereaved person, recognizing that people do not function optimally while grieving. During this year, the person's identity is that of a bereaved person.

But the focused grieving needs to come to an end so people can begin rebuilding their lives. A ceremony would acknowledge the loss and would point the bereaved person to the future. His or her identity would shift from the past to what lies ahead, and there is a new commitment to life.

ACCEPTING RESPONSIBILITY FOR ONE'S GRANDCHILDREN

A man and woman in rural Georgia worked very hard to raise their three children. By the time the last one left home, they were exhausted, both personally and financially. Seven years later, the husband died.

One of the daughters had great difficulty getting her life together. A serious drug abuser, she had two children outside of marriage, with no support from the male biological progenitors. (I prefer this term to the word "father." To me, "father" has to do with commitment and love, not genetics.) The children were tragically neglected and sometimes abused. When the male progenitor of one of the children tried to get custody, the child's mother realized she could not care for these children and took them to her own mother to raise.

There were several problems: How could the grandmother find the extra income necessary to raise two disturbed children? How would she deal with the biological progenitor who was trying to get custody? Where could she find the energy to handle these children? How could she enlist help from other people? How could she forgive her daughter for messing up both their lives in this manner?

A ceremony might acknowledge the difficult situation she was in, affirm her choices, and promise the support of her community.

SUPPORT FOR A SURVIVOR OF ETHNIC CLEANSING

An increasing number of refugees in the United States have come from countries where ethnic cleansing has claimed friends and members of their families. The survivors bring with them many conflicting feelings. On the one hand, it is very difficult to get beyond the terror that someone will yet kill them or other loved ones. The world is still experienced as senselessly dangerous, with attendant feelings of confusion, anxiety, and insecurity.

Often, those who were killed are seen as more deserving of life than those who survived. The survivors often feel a great sense of shame and guilt. At a very deep level of their psyche, they feel terribly isolated and alone.

A ceremony would address all these issues. It would help people forgive themselves for surviving. It would provide a context in which people could remember and grieve, and then reconnect with family and community.

MARKING THE END OF AN AFFAIR

One young pastor, during a time of great stress, had become romantically involved with a college student in his church. When he finally "came to himself" (as did the prodigal son), he was horrified at what he had done. He asked his therapist to find some special way to affirm his determination never to do such a thing again.

The therapist suggested a kind of ceremony for new beginnings. Interestingly, the client himself wrote this ceremony for the therapist to conduct.* He understood the power of ceremonial language.

The ceremony included these comments:

"The road of life is not a highway, straight and paved, with clear signs along the way telling you what to do and how to get to where you are going. In many ways, it is an unbroken trail. Other people have made their way through similar trails, but none exactly duplicates yours. This means that there will be many mistakes along the way.

"Sometimes people have to go down a dead-end road before they realize that it leads nowhere. It often takes something very painful to push them to find and to appreciate the depths of our psyche. . . .

---

*I remember a client for whom I had written an allegory. When I read it to her, she felt it needed improvement. So she took it home and rewrote parts of it. The next week, she brought it to the office for me to read again. To my surprise, she wept while I was reading it!

"Affairs are always more fun than marriages. They are based on people's images of themselves and the other. So the relationship is imaginary—image related. When people have to share responsibilities, these images tend to dissipate."

The therapist told the client that negative feelings such as guilt and shame should be appreciated. They are the psyche's effort to keep us from making other mistakes. He should keep as much guilt and shame as he needed to monitor his behavior until other more mature motivations took their place.

The young man had also written a letter to himself, and he gave the sealed envelope to his therapist to keep for him.

There are probably a number of books which, like this one, are collections of ceremonies for healing and growth, but I do not know of any. You may find some references in Herbert Anderson and Edward Foley's book *Mighty Stories, Dangerous Rituals* (1997). If you run across books of ceremonies, or if you create any yourselves, I would be most grateful if you would let me know.

Appendix A

Guided Meditation for Spiritual Growth

A middle-aged woman told me during a therapy session that she wanted to cultivate the dimension of spirituality in her life. After talking with her for some time about what that might entail, I invited her into a meditative state and said something such as this, speaking slowly and softly (you will get a better "feel" of this meditation if you read it aloud, slowly and softly):

"I would like for you to visit in your imagination some place that is sacred for you, maybe a church, maybe the church you knew as a child, maybe a chapel of some kind, maybe a small chapel in a forest or by a lake, maybe a nature scene that feels sacred to you, maybe a mountaintop, where you can witness the grandeur of nature, maybe a more intimate setting such as sitting on a rock beside a stream and feeling at one with the world around you, maybe in a garden, surrounded by reminders of the beauty and mystery of life, maybe at a beach beside the ocean, letting yourself experience the immensity and also the nearness of that which is the womb from which all of life has come, maybe someplace else, but let yourself visit some place that is sacred for you; let yourself become one with that place, feeling its goodness, feeling its presence there for you, really putting yourself in that place and the feelings and attitudes that characterize your presence there.

"As you are there, you can gradually become aware of God being there with you—as you understand God—to protect you, to protect your privacy, to let you set your own pace for what you experience. And then let a scene unfold that is appropriate to your own inner self and to your understanding of God. One way the scene might unfold is that you would gradually become aware of a dim light at a particular spot in the heavens, and the very faint strains of very quiet, beautiful music.

"As the music gradually increases in volume and intensity and meaning, you are aware that something is being lowered from the heavens—perhaps something like a holy grail, covered by a veil that transmits a soft glow of light. You watch with peace and expectation as it draws nearer and the music builds to a brilliant crescendo. At that moment, the veil is lifted from the grail and its transcendent light shines forth for a long and beautiful moment,

doi:10.1300/5590_20

129

and you feel profoundly at one with the light and the music and the holy grail and with God and with all things.*

"Then gradually the music begins to fade, the grail is gently covered and begins to ascend into the heavens, and slowly and quietly leaves you with a sense that something new has been awakened in you, something that feels very familiar and at the same time profoundly new and different, something that can lead to some significant changes in your own life. You may wonder what those changes will be. How will they affect your inner life? Or the world of your relationships? What will be the first of those changes that you might notice? Will it be easier for you to forgive yourself for mistakes you have made? Will it be easier to deal with some of the terrible hurts you have suffered in the past?

"And what are some changes that other people might notice, maybe even before you do? You can be curious about those and many other things, with a deep sense of confidence, a deep sense of peace, a deep sense of quietness. . . . And in a few moments, when you have reoriented yourself, I would be glad to hear about any part of that experience that you might want to share with me, and I will certainly respect any parts of it that you want to keep all to yourself."

Nicole cried softly during much of the time I was talking, and continued for a few moments afterward. She then thanked me warmly and told me she knew the directions she needed to take.

A similar approach was used with a woman whose husband and teenage son had recently become born-again Christians and were badgering her to do so as well, to "surrender to Christ." She said that in some ways she really wanted to do that. It would enable her to let go of some of the tensions and resentments that burdened her. But she certainly wasn't going to submit to the pressure of her family. She was also aware of her own passion to be in control of everything, and to surrender would be to give up that control.

After inviting her into a meditative state, to a place that was sacred for her, I suggested a kind of rehearsal. She could let one part of herself play a role, while another part of herself observed. The actress part of her would play out the experience of surrendering to Christ, which I described in elaborate detail as I thought *she* understood it. The observing part of her would videotape this experience. When it had been accomplished, the observer part of her would rejoin the actress part of her and give her the videotape so that if and when she wanted to take this step, she would have a sense of what was involved.

---

*Pianist Loren Hollander said that for great artists, it was like a curtain had been pulled back, just for a moment, and they glimpsed the eternal. Their astonished reaction was a breathless, "Oh my God! This is what is real!" They were then pushed back—almost unwillingly—into the mundane realities of this world, to bear witness to what they had experienced.

Appendix B

Pastoral Care for an Unconscious Person

Jean was a woman in her early fifties with no family, few friends, and very limited resources. Her church supplemented her meager disability income to help her live independently.

She had been struggling with cancer for several years, and now felt death was imminent. A few months earlier, chemotherapy had been discontinued since it was accomplishing nothing. Jean was in constant pain and was impatient to die. She could no longer drive, so she asked me to come to her apartment for our occasional visits.

One day, it took her a long time to get to the door. When she finally opened it, she looked terrible: face emaciated, hair disheveled, wearing a rumpled nightie, shaking convulsively every few seconds.

I was afraid she would collapse on the floor, so I seized her shoulders firmly and helped her back to the couch where she had been lying. The trip to the door and back had absolutely exhausted her, and she gasped for breath while her body continued to convulse.

My immediate goal with Jean was to help her relax. A longer-term goal was to help make the process of dying as easy as possible.

(❧)

I sat down at the end of the couch and spoke slowly and softly, timing my phrases with her exhaling.

Speaking in unison with another's breathing is a powerful means of creating rapport. There are at least two ways of understanding this. The first has to do with the interplay of the conscious and the unconscious activities of the mind. Breathing is a function of the subconscious mind; speaking is a function of the conscious mind. When these two function together, in syn-

---

This appendix is adapted from my article "Pastoral Care for an Unconscious Person," *The Journal of Pastoral Care and Counseling,* Vol. 52, No. 2, Summer 1998, and is used with the publisher's permission.

chronization, it creates a sense of wholeness and security. It facilitates a sense of peace.

Also, I speak when I am exhaling. If I time this to match the client's exhaling, then we are breathing in synchronization. At a bodily level, we are in rapport.

When Gregory Bateson was dying, he went to a Zen monastery in San Francisco for his final days. The monks, apparently drawing on an ancient custom, would take turns sitting beside his bed and breathing in synchronization with him.

Try it with your children sometime. Toward the end of your bedtime story, speak slower and softer, and in shorter phrases that are in unison with their breathing. One of Milton Erickson's children said of this approach, "Mommy talks us to sleep, but Daddy breathes us to sleep."

"You look like you have had a really hard day, Jean. And now you are resting quietly on the couch."

Speaking a person's name frequently is an important means of rapport. I do this with people who are awake as well as with people who are asleep, unconscious, or in a hypnotic state. Several people have told me this was very supportive to them.

An experiment in a California mental hospital is relevant to this. All the patients were randomly assigned to various therapy groups. Leadership of these groups was then assigned to *all* the staff—including secretaries, cooks, and janitors. The sessions were taped and then evaluated by laypeople.

Patients seemed to benefit from all these groups. In fact, patients in groups led by low-status people (janitors and cooks) actually did better than those led by professionals. When the laypeople analyzed the group interactions, the biggest difference they noticed was the frequency with which the janitors and cooks used the patients' names!

Even the imagined use of a person's name has power. One client said that in a dream, she had changed into a dog. She ran down to the creek to find me. When I addressed her by her name, she turned back into a person.

"Your eyes are closed. Your head is on the pillow. Your breathing is labored right now, but it may become easier in just a few moments."

Rapport is also enhanced by commenting on the obvious. It conveys a sense of acceptance and affirmation. "I really am in touch with you, listening, observing, acknowledging, accepting."

It also elicits a sense of agreement. That may lead to the person being more open to suggestions I might make later, such as the suggestion to relax.

"You can let yourself relax very comfortably. No need to be aware of my presence. No need to listen to my words. The subconscious mind has its own ways of listening, and remembering, and finding [note the shift from describing to suggesting] something useful in what is said. Your subconscious mind is always working for your best interest. No need to think about anything. Just let yourself enter very deeply into a state of relaxation and peace."

Pastoral care for the unconscious person is based on the principle that the subconscious mind is always active, even when the conscious mind is decommissioned. The sense of hearing remains active, even after other senses have been totally suppressed.

A growing body of evidence shows that patients hear and react to things said to them when they are unconscious. Even in the operating room, under anesthesia, patients react. If for instance a doctor makes some pessimistic or derogatory comment about the patient, his or her pulse rate may increase.

Operating room memories are not usually accessible when the patient is in the ordinary waking state. But when the anesthetized state is replicated, say by hypnosis, patients can report detailed conversations that took place around them.

This has profound implications for pastoral care. When a patient is unconscious, he or she will be *more* receptive to our input rather than less. This receptivity is at a subconscious level rather than the more superficial conscious level. The defenses and rationalizations of the conscious mind are not at work monitoring what I say. The person is simply listening.

When I am in dialogue with someone, half of my mental energy goes into listening and understanding. The other half is focused on creating an effective response. If there is no expectation of a response, I can listen with my whole self.

Dr. Milton Erickson did much of his therapy while patients were in a hypnotic state—and sometimes when he himself was in a hypnotic state. He felt that patients who did not remember what took place tended to benefit more than those who remembered.

The renowned family therapist John Weakland told me that he saw Dr. Erickson for an extended session of hypnotherapy once. He had no memory of what was said, but was aware of some significant changes in his life during the next few years.

When a spasm racked Jean's body, I said, "I am aware of your muscles twitching. You have spoken often, Jean, of your wish to die soon. Maybe that twitching of the muscles is the dance of letting go. Maybe it is the dance of moving on to a happier world, moving on to a happier life, moving into a deeper state of comfort and well-being."

When another spasm would occur, I would say, "That's it. Just let your body express itself in any way it wishes. Let it dance that dance of letting go. Let each one of those twitches lead you into a deeper sense of peace and relaxation. Let each one of those twitches create its own kind of comfort."

I gave Jean very few direct suggestions. Instead, I presented options. "You can . . ." or "You may . . ." or "Maybe . . ." This implied that she had options and had the power to choose among them.

I do my best to speak from within the other person's worldview, even if it is different from my own. Under no circumstances would I try to change it. To try to "convert" someone would be an abuse of power, an exploitation of the person's vulnerability. It would create anxiety, and would surely arouse resentment and contempt.

When people are distressed, it may seem that there is no alternative to the pain and suffering. To talk about other possibilities gently challenges that assumption and invites people into those different mind-sets. They may understand subconsciously that the ability to relax comfortably is an option that is open to them.

The principle of reframing was also used. When people are distressed, things beyond their control are often frightening. I assumed this was true of Jean's convulsions. So I defined them as the twitching of her muscles. To normalize one's distress can be very comforting and supportive. I suggested that the twitching could serve the purpose of leading her into a state of relaxation. I also related it to her stated wish to die.

In this same spirit, I never mentioned pain. Instead, I spoke of comfort and well-being.

If I comment on something, I give it reality and importance. If I do not comment on it, I minimize its reality. I wanted Jean to focus on memories of peace and comfort, not on the present experience of discomfort.

I then spoke of several things related to the process of dying, continuing to synchronize my phrases with her exhaling. I regarded this as a kind of prayer, although it lacked the usual formal language.

I reminded Jean—with great elaboration—that every stage of life has its own responsibilities, its own challenges, its own rewards. I then repeated to her some of the things I had told another friend a few years earlier (see Appendix C).

The convulsions had quickly become less intense and less frequent. I still commented on each of them as a means of entering more deeply into a state of relaxation and peace. During this whole time, Jean would moan frequently, but she said absolutely nothing. After about forty minutes she was resting comfortably in a very deep sleep.

The concept of utilization is central to this approach to pastoral care. *Everything* is a potential source of healing and growth. These resources are in our memory banks. Some are memories of things we have learned and accomplished. Some are abilities, such as the ability to create things in our imagination. Even symptoms (such as convulsions) can be used in the healing process.

When I talk about those resources, I help make them more available to the present situation. If I then talk about the area of need, I juxtapose these two realities. I may even talk about how one is related to the other. In this way, I help build bridges between resources and areas of need.

When I asked Jean to create events in her imagination, I was drawing on an ability I assumed she possessed. I then used that ability to help bring a peaceful closure to her life.

I also spoke of her dying as part of the continuum of life, the final chapter of a process. It had a purpose, a challenge. It could be approached calmly and peacefully.

As I prepared to leave, I said, "Now in a few moments, I'm going to be leaving, Jean. I would like for you to keep on sleeping, keep on relaxing, keep on visiting happy memories. No need to say good-bye to me, no need to acknowledge my leaving. No need even to remember that I have been here. Just remember how to create a sense of well-being. And you can use my leaving as an occasion to enter even more deeply into a state of peace and relaxation."

When I stood to leave, Jean seemed absolutely unaware of it. She continued to sleep deeply as I let myself out.

I would have not been surprised if Jean had died while I was there. I fully expected her to die that afternoon. But she lived another couple of weeks, and I was able to see her once more. I think my ministry helped her to die more gracefully and peacefully.

⟨᷉⟩

When I was in training some two and a half paradigms ago, pastoral care was taught as a responsive activity. The patient or parishioner would say something, and the pastor would respond. Our ministry was to convey understanding and to help the person find constructive meanings in the situations and events of his or her life. Since an unconscious person could not talk, this model for pastoral care did not apply. Not once during my academic and clinical training was there a single reference to the pastoral care of an unconscious person.

This approach emphasized rational processes; it was expressed primarily in the form of ideas. Today, we would understand it as an activity primarily of the left hemisphere of the brain.

A right-brain approach would emphasize nurture rather than analysis. It is not oriented to ideas, but rather to feelings, meditation, imagination, and metaphor. It also emphasizes the initiative of the pastor, not just his or her responses.

Some years ago, I was seriously ill for a month or so. I had no energy for anything. My worst dread was that friends would come to visit me. I would have had to greet them, talk with them, look at them, and pretend I appreciated their coming. I did not have the energy for any of that. I wanted to be left alone.

Even so, I would have welcomed a visit from someone who would have simply stroked my arm and talked to me without expecting any response.

In my ministry to seriously distressed people, I want to be a source of energy, not a drain. This often requires that I be the one to initiate everything.

My friend Tricia Senterfitt sometimes sings to patients who are in a coma. When she has sung to Alzheimer's patients, they have often joined her in the singing—even people who have not spoken in months.

❧

These principles are also relevant to other situations.

Louise is a woman I met at a church retreat several years ago. She and her husband and I became good friends. During the past several years, Louise had undergone four surgeries for some complex difficulty. One more extensive operation was needed, which would be very hard on her physically and emotionally.

The day before the surgery, I visited her. As I sat next to the bed, I asked if she would like for me to hold her hand, or if that would be a distraction. She wanted to hold my hand. I told her my hand could symbolize the hands of all her friends and loved ones, who now supported her with their love and prayers. The touch of my hand could symbolize the touch of Jesus' hand, which brought healing and well-being.

If it would be inappropriate to hold the person's hand, I might comment on my presence or my voice symbolizing the presence or the voice of family and friends.

Next, I invited Louise into a state of relaxation, as I had done with Jean. I then talked at length about the inner self and the many memories that the inner self holds dear.

"Now as you know, there are different parts of the mind that memorize different kinds of things. There is a part of the mind that memorizes numbers, like telephone numbers or the multiplication table. You draw on those memories when you need them. There is another part of the mind that memorizes sounds, like the sound of a loved one's voice, or the sound of a piece of music. You draw on those memories when you need them.

"There is a part of the mind that memorizes appearances, like a familiar tree near your home, or a painting that you and Ed have enjoyed together. You draw on those memories when you need them. There is a part of your mind that memorizes feelings. Memorize feelings of relaxation. Memorize feelings of comfort. Memorize feelings of well-being. Memorize the feelings that contribute to healing and to comfort. And draw on those memories when you need them. [These last few sentences are framed so they are suggestions rather than descriptions.]

"Maybe there is a place that symbolizes comfort and well-being. You can visit that place in your imagination, savor its goodness, and relive the happy memories that are associated with it.

"You have also had many experiences when you have forgotten things. You have sometimes forgotten people's names. There have been times when you couldn't remember the name of a song or certain things on your shopping list.

"It is very nice to forget things sometimes. When you were a little girl playing with your friends, there were times when you would fall down and hurt yourself—bump your elbow or skin your knee. That would hurt so bad! But you would see your friends waiting for you, and would get up to go on playing with them. In just a few moments, you would forget all about the hurt. Your attention would be with your friends and the good time you were having together. I think that is a wonderful skill—the ability to forget. It is a skill that can serve you very well.

"Now of course pain is a moment-to-moment experience. Anybody can deal with a momentary experience of pain, no matter how terrible it is. [This first reference to pain described it as severe. Later references would refer to pain in more casual terms—such as "discomfort."] When you experience that moment of pain, that would be a wonderful time to draw on your ability to forget. You can draw on those wonderful experiences of forgetfulness that you have learned throughout your life. How good and pleasant it is, Louise, simply to enjoy forgetting, to enjoy forgetting your body, to enjoy forgetting your surroundings, to enjoy forgetting any momentary experience of discomfort.

"From one moment to the next, it is a simple matter to remember to forget. Remember to remember things that are important, such as the healing you are experiencing, and let yourself forget—well, you may not even remember what it is that you are forgetting. Your attention can be on remembering the people who love you and support you, and bring you energy and health. Make good use of your selective memory while you are here, and throughout your life. . . ."

While I was talking, a nurse came in to hook up some tubes and adjust her IV. I told Louise she could use the presence of the nurse to let herself enter even more deeply into a state of deep relaxation and recuperation. She appeared to be totally oblivious to the nurse's presence.

I then mentioned that in healing, the cells at the point of an incision become very active. They reach out to other cells to interlock with them and thus to create healing. "This happens in relationships also. All your many friends and loved ones are reaching out in a kind of interlocking that surrounds you with their love and their energy and their support of the healing processes that are active in your body and your psyche."

I then reminded her that she has had many experiences where her body created healing following an illness or an injury or an operation. And the bodily memories of how to do that are still with her, in her subconscious mind. And the power of those memories is still available to her. She can remember and make use of those memories, letting those memories have power with her.

"There may also be memories that are painful. Maybe something here in the hospital will trigger some of those memories. That's all right. Just remember those things long enough to file them away to address at some appropriate time in the future."

After Louise returned home, she said the only thing she remembered about my visit was my hand symbolizing the touch of Jesus' hand. But something surprising had happened. Following each of her other surgeries, she had suffered severe nausea for a couple days. This time there was none. She attributed that to our work together.

If the setting had been different, I might have smiled with a twinkle in my eye and said something playful. "Don't ever forget that! Just remember that you are eternally obligated to me for the rest of your life!"

But this was not a time for playfulness, so I told her that any credit for that was hers, not mine. If she can take a few words that somebody says and let them have that kind of power with her, that is her accomplishment.

⌇∾⌇

If I were visiting in the hospital someone whom I did not know, and he or she was asleep, I might say something such as this while I was still a few steps away from the bed.

"I would like for you to continue to rest comfortably. No need to open your eyes. No need to wake up. My name is Henry Close. I'm the chaplain here, and I've come to be with you for a few moments."

By speaking while I am still a few steps away from the bed, my words are part of the background. They do not call for a response. After I have said that the patient does not need to acknowledge me, then I can introduce myself, move in a little closer, and decide whether to sit down. I would then continue, speaking nonchalantly.

"You are now here in the hospital for a few days. It is a time for recovery and healing. And of course there have been other times in your life when you have experienced healing. And your inner self remembers how that healing

took place—memories that we can't understand with the conscious mind. But just as the subconscious mind understands how to grow, how to breathe, and how to digest food, so the subconscious mind knows how to create healing and well-being."

My first wish would be to soften the patient's anxieties. My nonchalance and my comment that hospitalization will be for only a few days would be designed to minimize the severity of the situation. By relating healing to such common things as breathing and digesting food, I would imply that this healing is easily available. If I knew certain things about the patient, I would of course try to weave these into my comments.

This kind of pastoral care comes from a different area of the psyche than the pastoral care that takes place in dialogue. It also brings a different kind of satisfaction. The patient may not tell me how much he or she appreciated my visit, since she or he may not even remember it. But I will know in my heart that I have done something worthwhile.

Appendix C

Ministry to a Dying Person

When a person approaches death, several themes can be helpfully addressed by a pastor, therapist, and/or friend: normalizing the experience of death and accepting its reality, addressing possible guilt and shame, dealing with unresolved issues and relationships, entrusting the memories of one's life to loved ones, saying good-bye, letting go. As at other times in one's life, things such as these are addressed more convincingly and with more power and grace if they are addressed metaphorically.

This is especially true of experiences of guilt and shame. If I tell someone, "All your 'sins' [whatever that means for a particular person] have been forgiven," that will sound trite and insulting. But certain metaphors can address that kind of thing powerfully and without insult.

Ellen was a member of the church where I am minister of counseling. She was a really exceptional and beautiful human being. I had known her and her husband fairly well prior to the diagnosis of cancer. During the last months of her illness, I saw her weekly for supportive pastoral care, using guided meditation and imagery. I would sit next to the bed, hold her hand, and stroke her arm for a few moments (I would not have done this had we not been old friends), and then talk about things related to the process of dying.

I made sure my manner was straightforward and warm, rather than somber. I made a point of speaking her name frequently, which she said was particularly supportive to her. These were beautifully tender and intimate experiences for me. I felt she gave me access to a deep part of her soul, as I did for her. I am writing this report out of my deep respect and affection for her, and as a way of finishing my own process of saying good-bye.

Ellen's worldview was that of a conservative Christian, so I spoke from that perspective as sensitively as I could. I also made her an audiotape, in which I repeated many of the things I had said in person.

This appendix is adapted from my book *Metaphor in Psychotherapy*, Chapter 22, and is used with the publisher's permission. Ellen's family has read this chapter and agreed to its publication.

doi:10.1300/5590_22

I sometimes began some of the early sessions with some variation of the following, speaking slowly and softly in very short phrases, in synchronization with her exhaling. If you will read this aloud, slowly and softly, you will get a better "feel" of what I was trying to convey.

"I would like to invite you, Ellen, to get in a really comfortable position, letting yourself take a couple of deep breaths, and relax quietly, letting your attention focus on the inner self, letting your subconscious mind be attentive to anything that can promote comfort and healing and strength.

"You may want to let your eyes close gently, or you may find that they will close all by themselves as we progress. There is no need to listen to me with the conscious mind, or even to be aware of my presence. To listen with the conscious self requires energy, and you don't need to do that. The subconscious mind can listen and understand without any effort, without any need to respond, without any expenditure of energy.

"You might want to give yourself a visual image of a place that represents healing and well-being for you, maybe a nature scene, maybe a beach at the ocean or a lake, with the colors of water and sky and background, the wonderfully invigorating sense of breeze and fragrance. Maybe it will be a mountain or a valley, maybe a garden or a stream, with all the sensations of color and pattern, the warmth of the sun on your face or the coolness of the breeze on your skin, the sounds of a running stream or of birds singing in the distance, and everything else that may accompany that experience, putting yourself into that place to feel its peace, its security, its healing." (Notice the different senses that were addressed: sight, sound, smell, and touch. Notice also the permissive nature of all these comments. I never actually told her to do anything. By my tone of voice as well as through my words, I simply presented options and invited her to experience them. This approach is similar to the approach to hypnosis pioneered by Milton H. Erickson.)

As I would get ready to leave, I would tell that her that I was going to leave soon. She was welcome to keep my presence with her in any way she wanted. When I said good-bye, I wanted her to remain in a state of deep relaxation and peace. She did not need to say good-bye or acknowledge my leaving in any way. She could just continue to relax comfortably.

☙

On one occasion, I reminded Ellen that every stage of life has its own responsibilities, its own challenges, its own rewards. When she was an infant, she faced the many challenges of becoming more independent—learning to walk, to feed herself, to communicate, to relate to other children. As those tasks were accomplished, she felt a growing sense of pride and competence.

As a teenager, she laid the foundations for her adult life, preparing for a career, choosing the partner with whom she would share her life. With these accomplishments came a growing sense of being her own person, able to make the important decisions about her life, and finding many moments of deep joy.

As a young adult, she married and had three exceptional children. She invested herself in the task of building a family—of learning to be a wife and mother as well as enriching her own sense of being a loving person. She especially wanted to avoid some of the mistakes her parents had made in raising her.

In middle age, she came to understand God in a much deeper and more personal way, an understanding of the heart more than just the mind, and felt a deepening of her sense of being a truly spiritual person.

As her children left home to establish their own careers and begin their own families, she gained a sense of being part of the broader flow of life, from father to son to grandson, from mother to daughter to granddaughter, as one generation gives birth and meaning and purpose to another generation, and then another. She feels herself as an integral part of the whole fabric of life—not just her own family, but also the family of humanity.

"Now the final chapter is beginning to unfold. This is a time for stepping back and reviewing one's life. It is a time for reflection and celebration. To be sure, there are some other challenges as well: letting go of things that are peripheral, forgiving oneself and other people, saying good-byes. But basically, it is a time for reflection and celebration. And in many ways, you have done that beautifully, setting aside time with your family to remember happy times you have shared together, and by the remembering, affirming, and celebrating yourself and your life.

"There will be some specific memories of times when you were loved, of times when you really felt cherished and loved, maybe at a time when you might not have felt particularly lovable. But someone who was important to you saw beneath the surface and reached out to you in a beautiful kind of tenderness and affirmation. You felt an inner glow as you basked in the warmth of that person's love and appreciation for you. You felt good and strong inside. There may be a specific memory that comes to mind. As you relive that memory, you can put yourself again into that memory, savor its goodness, feel its power, know its deep meanings for you in the present."

I then told her about an epitaph that read, "I'm deeply grateful to God for the privilege of having lived." I thought that would be true for her, and also for her family. They too would be grateful for her life.

On another occasion, I talked about the untold thousands of memories that are part of anyone's life, memories of many different kinds of things. "Many of these memories are happy, tender memories. Other memories may be sad, or even painful. It's like we have these memories filed away in our minds under various categories, almost like filing cabinets with different memories in different drawers.

"If someone asks me to recall a happy memory from the time my children were little, I can do that. I go to that drawer and retrieve a memory.

"Many of our memories can fit just as well in a different category from the one in which they were originally filed. During this final chapter of life, it is appropriate to revisit many of those memories, reevaluate them, and refile them.

"There may be a memory, for instance, of a terribly embarrassing incident. As you reflect on that memory, you may realize that your own embarrassment helped you be even more sensitive to other people's feelings. So that memory should be refiled under 'Helpful Learning Experiences' rather than under 'Embarrassing Memories.'

"Another memory may be of a time when you really treated someone shabbily, and you have carried a burden of guilt about that for a long time. As you review that memory, you may commit it to God. Then you can file it once and for all under 'Things for Which I Have Been Forgiven,' and let go of the guilt. Maybe a memory from the 'Stupid Mistakes' drawer can be refiled under the category 'Experiences that Reminded Me of My Humanness.'

"During this final chapter of your life's drama, there will be many opportunities to review memories, and make sure they are filed appropriately. You know that in the eyes of God, 'appropriate' means 'with love and forgiveness'—always. Because the ways of God are different from the ways of the world.

"In some ways, one's life is like a portrait, a living portrait. Throughout the days of our lives, we keep adding a bit here and a bit there, every event eventually becoming part of the background. After a time, many of the events recede way back out of focus, providing a setting on which the foreground is built.

"Periodically the perspective of the portrait changes. You can see and understand the background differently, the processes differently; you see and understand your own self differently. With each event in your life, you enrich this portrait, sometimes changing the focus, sometimes adding important new qualities, sometimes de-emphasizing one area so that you can highlight another.

"Not all of the pigments are bright and colorful. There are certainly many dark areas in anyone's life. Some of those dark times are of pain that had to be endured, 'valleys of the shadow of death' that had to be traversed. Some of them depict times of loss, of grief, of letting go. Some may represent mistakes that were made, maybe serious mistakes. But these mistakes ultimately helped you to choose more wisely the kind of person you wanted to be, the kind of life you wanted to live. So in that sense even those dark areas can be appreciated and celebrated.

"There are also many cheerful, joyful aspects to this portrait, many memories that still bring a smile and a deep sense of satisfaction. Each memory, each scene of the portrait can be thought of as a gift. Maybe the gift was an affirmation from a friend or loved one. Maybe the gift was something that led you—or maybe pushed you—to a deeper sense of your own inner self. Maybe many other kinds of gifts of the Spirit cannot be named or described, but can only be accepted by the heart.

"Some areas of the portrait are clear and precise; others are more diffuse, nebulous. Some learnings may have been harder to come by. But now you can step back and review the whole painting. You may look at one incident that is part of the background, smile warmly, and think to yourself, 'I'm so grateful for that.' There may be another incident in which you really felt good about what you said and did. You can say to yourself, 'I hope my family and my friends never forget that.'

"There may be other scenes that are part of the background of that portrait. Some are of times when you really felt loved, when someone truly and deeply loved you, and you felt blessed. There may be other scenes in which you felt very close to God. You were in touch with your own spirituality and felt a sense of wholeness, of being at peace with yourself and the whole world, where you felt an authentic joy in the depth of your soul.

"As the closing pages of this final chapter approach, then it is time to say good-bye. You can visit in your imagination many of the places, the events, the things, the people that have been important to you, and say good-bye to them with warmth and appreciation.

"There may be special places you have always enjoyed being—maybe a room in your home, maybe a church, maybe a place you have visited on vacations—that hold some very special memories for you. You can visit those places again in your imagination. Let yourself experience again the pleasures of being there, and with a warm smile, say good-bye to those places.

"There may be some certain things that are very special to you, maybe a tree you planted in your yard, maybe a gift someone gave you, maybe something one of your children made for you, maybe something else. Take that item into your consciousness now, let yourself appreciate it anew, maybe imagine yourself touching it and saying, 'Thank you for the pleasures you have brought me,' as you say good-bye.

"There are certain events that live in your memory. You can put yourself back into those events, experience them anew as you say your good-byes. And of course there are the people who have been important to you and to whom you have been important. You can let yourself do a leisurely review of many of those people who have been part of your life. There may be something special you will want to say to each one of them in your good-byes, something special each of them will say to you, maybe in words, maybe even more so in the expression on their faces or the warmth of their embrace.

"Finally there may be some special things you have said or done that seem to capture the essence of the 'you' that you want people to remember. Take some time to revisit those special moments. You can smile as you look into the future to a time when your husband is remembering a moment that you and he have shared, and he breathes a prayer of gratitude for you. Or you can take great pleasure in visiting a time in the future when one of your children remembers something about you and smiles to himself or herself and says, 'I'm glad I had a mother like that.'

"So this final chapter of life has its own unique responsibilities, challenges, opportunities, gratifications. When the time comes for that chapter to be closed, you entrust the memories of yourself, the 'portrait' of your life, to the loving care of your family, and entrust yourself to the loving care of God."

☙

I then told Ellen of the patient whose daughter and four grandchildren had been burned to death (see Chapter 17). She had talked about feeling trapped in a room with a huge piece of ice blocking the door. She would rub on the ice with her hands to try to melt some of it away, but she could rub for only a little while because her hands got so cold.

She would leave the ice and do some other things for a while, rubbing her hands together to get them warm again. Then she would go back to the ice and rub some more. Finally she had melted away enough of the ice so there was a hole big enough for her to crawl out of.

"Unfortunately, Ellen, your friends cannot rub the ice for you, nobody else has access to it. But what your friends *can* do is help you get your hands warm again. They can hold your hands gently against their heart, to let you feel their love for you."

Ellen interrupted me to say, "As you are doing for me."

I nodded, "Yes, as I am doing for you. I'm holding your hands lovingly next to my heart to help them to get warm."

☙

In March, Ellen had been told she had a month or so to live, maybe two at the most. She very much wanted to live through June, when her oldest son would graduate from medical school. It was a great joy when she *attended* the graduation. Then she wanted to live through July, when a son who was a missionary in Japan would be able to visit. That too was a happy gift for her. Then she wanted to live through September, when a daughter in Hawaii would give birth to her first granddaughter. But holding on was getting harder and harder.

One day early in September she told me she had had a terrible two weeks. I told her that the time would come when she would want me to talk about letting go, just as in the past she had wanted me to talk about holding on. She told me she thought that time was coming very soon. I asked if she would like me to talk on this day about letting go. She nodded.

I took her hand and stroked her arm, as I usually did. Speaking very slowly and softly, I then took her on an elaborate imaginary trip to visit the daughter in Hawaii. I talked about how the ocean is the womb from which all life has come, and how appropriate that the island of Hawaii is surrounded by the ocean. I pointed out the changes in the color and texture of the ocean as we flew over the reefs, the beauty and power of the surf as it crashed against the rocky coast, the beauty and majesty of the mountains in the distance.

"When we land at the airport, we are met by your daughter and son-in-law, who drive you to their home. You can take particular pleasure in the beautiful flowers you see along the way [Ellen loved flowers]—flowers and trees and shrubs that are very different from those here in Atlanta: orchids, bromeliads, antheriums, hibiscus, all a glorious burst of color and design and splendor. The trees are different too, different shades of color, shapes, textures, leaf formations, all speaking of the tremendous goodness and variety of life.

"You can also be interested in the beautiful birds you see and hear as you drive through the neighborhood. Hawaii is known for its spectacular, colorful birds, and their beautiful singing, and it will be like they are singing just for you.

"When you arrive at your daughter's home, you will greet your two grandsons, who adore you. You will enjoy a wonderful afternoon with the whole family, reminiscing and celebrating your life together. Then later on, it will be time to go to the birthing center. Your daughter's husband will stand on one side, and you on the other, holding your daughter's hands as she gives birth. She has a very easy delivery, so you can devote your whole attention to the beautiful little girl who is being born.

"I don't know whether you will look first at your daughter, and the pride you will feel for her and the joy you will feel as you see her joy. Or maybe you will look first at the baby, noticing everything about her—whom she looks like, the color of her hair, how she wiggles her hands and feet, what kinds of sounds she makes. Your own mother once looked on you with that same sense of mystery and awe, as you yourself have done with your own daughter.

"Baby will be washed and given to your daughter, who will hold her warmly for a while. Then she will give Baby to her husband, who will hold her in his own special way. Then he will hand Baby to you. You will hold Baby warmly next to your own body, to let Baby feel the warmth of your body and the pulse of your heart, and hear the sound of your voice. You will feel a tremendous glow of love radiating from your heart as you hold this new life in your arms. You may even be aware of tears in your eyes.

"You will know you are surrounding this baby not only with love and warmth, but with the deepest qualities of your soul. You will bestow on her a kind of blessing that cannot be put into words, but that she will know, and will feel, and will keep with her for her entire life. You have a special gift to give her that no one else can give—the gift of courage in the face of hard times. By the way you have lived these past few months, you have proclaimed that no matter how hard life is, life is worthwhile.

"Like any other human being, Baby will have some hard times to go through. But she will go through them with a deep-seated realization that she carries the blessing not only of her parents, but in a special way she carries the blessing of Grandmother for her first granddaughter, a grandmother who has modeled courage and determination. You can feel yourself loving and blessing this child, planting the seeds of those values and perspectives that have sustained you throughout your own life.

"After a little while, when it feels like the blessing has been fully bestowed, it is time to give Baby back to her mother, and for you to step back with a deep satisfaction. Your life has now had a wonderful culmination, a wonderful fulfillment, and it is all right to let go.

"As you begin to let go, you can be aware of the people who have gone before you, and who will be waiting to greet you. [I emphasized this because research has shown that most rituals surrounding the processes of dying focus not on the bereaved, but on incorporating the dead person into the community of life that is beyond death.] Father will be there, along with your grandparents. They have been waiting for you for a long time.

"There will be other people there who have been important to you. Your brother will be there, aunts and uncles who may have been special to you, maybe cousins. There will also be friends there—your roommate from college, maybe a neighbor, maybe a pastor—people who have meant a lot to you in the course of your life, and people to whom you have meant a lot. They will especially want to greet you with their love and appreciation.

"I don't know how you will envision God and Jesus greeting you, but they will be there too. And then you can look forward to greeting the friends and loved ones who will come along later. They will all be along in due time. Mother will be there soon. Then your husband before too awfully long. I'll be there before too long, and will really look forward to your greeting me. And you can know that it is all right, that your life has come to its own beautiful conclusion. You have been privileged to be part of the flow of life from one generation to another, and now it is all right to let go.

"So you can now picture yourself flying back home. At an appropriate time, you may lie down in bed, call your husband and children and grandchildren—especially your new granddaughter—to come and be with you.

Maybe they will sit on the bed and hold your hand or caress your arm. You will tell them that you are ready to go now, and you entrust your life and your memories to them in loving appreciation. Then you might just say good-bye, and close your eyes quietly, and let go."

When I told Ellen's husband about this (and later about another) imaginary trip, he seemed particularly touched.

The next week it was obvious that death was near. I told her how glad I was that she had had the opportunity to visit her daughter in Hawaii and be there for the birth of her first granddaughter. I summarized the trip, and then talked with her again about saying good-bye and letting go.

⟆⟍⟍⟎

I saw her again four days later. Her husband said she had wanted to visit her mother one last time—she was an Alzheimer's patient in a nursing home in the small town where Ellen had grown up. But Ellen was far too weak for any kind of trip. So I took her on another elaborate imaginary trip to visit them.

I described the familiar drive through the serene countryside, pointing out as many of the features as I could think of, including a sailboat on the lake next to the highway. As we came to the house in which she had grown up, I asked her to notice the trees and flowers in the yard. Notice the familiar look of the house, the furnishings, the pictures on the wall, the smells emanating from the kitchen, maybe even a familiar creak of the floorboards.

Mother and Dad are both there, in good health, in full possession of their faculties. She will greet them warmly, and reminisce about happy memories they shared together. Then she will say her loving good-byes to them. She will look forward to seeing them again soon in another life.

I then described a leisurely and pleasant drive back home, which she enjoyed with the deep satisfaction of having said her final good-byes. I then talked at some length about her dying with a smile on her face, a smile in her heart, knowing how many smiles she had brought to other people.

As I said good-bye and started to leave, she opened her hands toward me, indicating that she wanted me to hug her. As I did, she said with great effort, "I love you."

It was only after I had left the room that the moisture in my eyes became tears.

Three days later she was in a coma. I repeated some of the things I had said to her earlier, confident that the subconscious mind still hears and registers what is said. That afternoon, her granddaughter was born in Hawaii, two weeks early. Her husband held the phone to her ear so she could hear her granddaughter's "voice." A few hours later, she died quietly.

A concert pianist once said that a musician does not memorize his music—that would be impossible. A piano concerto may have as many as 500,000 notes. There is no way anyone could memorize that. Instead, he takes the music into his soul, lets it become part of him, enriches it with his own personal qualities. Then in a performance, the music "sings itself through him."

My time with Ellen reminded me that this is true of pastoral care also. Pastoral care is not a "thing" to be dispensed, like dispensing aspirin, even if that ministry consists of great wisdom, sensitivity, and warmth. Pastoral care is a particular kind of relationship between persons who at least to some extent open their hearts to each other.

Most of the things I said to Ellen were unplanned. When I walked into her room, something came to life between us, and the words then sang themselves through me to her.

Appendix D

Letters from Santa

My ten-year-old niece Laura is totally charming: bright, outgoing, playful, with flaming red hair and a face full of freckles. But Laura is very self-conscious about her freckles. At our Thanksgiving gathering, she told me she didn't like them and wished they would go away.

I wanted to reassure her that her freckles were in no way a liability: they were one of the features that make her who she is. But I knew that direct straightforward reassurances are totally unconvincing. Those are what someone is supposed to say.

Indirect reassurance, on the other hand, such as the use of a story, can be much more effective. I remembered that Milton Erickson sometimes wrote therapeutic letters to children—letters that had a kind of metaphoric quality to them.

Such letters can be extremely effective ways to communicate. In a dialogue, half of one's energy goes into hearing what is said; the other half is involved in thinking of a reply, or perhaps preparing a defense. When reading a letter, one can postpone a reply, and thus devote one's entire energy to reading and understanding. It is much less likely to stir up defensiveness.

The first step in a letter to Laura would be to establish rapport. I needed to let her know that I took her seriously and really understood how horrible freckles can be. Then I could reframe the situation in some kind of positive way.

I thought of Santa, who symbolizes gentleness and love. A letter from Santa could address her concerns in a loving way, but it needed to do so obliquely. Direct assurance, even from Santa, would lack authenticity.

I thought of a letter within a letter: one to establish rapport, the other to reframe.

This appendix is adapted from my articles "Freckles," *The Journal of Pastoral Care and Counseling,* Fall 2001, and "Letters from Santa," *The Journal of Pastoral Care and Counseling,* Winter 2004-2005. Both are used with the publisher's permission.

Santa's Workshop
The North Pole
Elfuary 333, 2003

Dear Laura,

A little girl in Seattle wrote me a most interesting letter, and I want to ask your advice about how to answer it. She wrote:

Dear Santa,

What I want for Christmas is something I don't want. I mean, I don't like the freckles on my face. My brother teases me about them, and makes me cry.

Mom and Dad tell him to cut it out, and he does for a while, but then he teases me again. Sometimes Dad gets really mad at him and yells at him. But he always teases me again the next day.

Please take these freckles off my face, or else take away my mean old brother. I don't know why anybody ever has to have freckles anyhow, because they always get teased. Who invented freckles anyhow???

Love,
Cindy

I wrote her back that very afternoon. Here is what I said:

Dear Cindy,

My goodness, it seems that you have a real problem. I know it must feel terrible when your brother teases you, especially when he teases you about how you look.

I'm sorry, but I couldn't take your freckles away, even if I wanted to—which I don't. If I took your freckles away, I would have to take away all the freckles in the whole world. Just think of how terrible that would be.

All the stars would disappear, because stars are the sky's freckles.

Nobody would ever be able to have lights on their Christmas tree, because those lights are the Christmas tree's freckles.

And there wouldn't be any more specks of light in the ocean at night, because those specks of light are the ocean's freckles.

The world would be much less interesting if all the freckles were gone.

But what I can bring you for Christmas is a box of cinnamon cookies. Cinnamon is about the same color as freckles, and if you spilled some on your face, nobody would notice.

Love,
Santa

Please tell me what else I should tell Cindy.

Love,
Santa

Cindy hated her freckles, and for good reason. If Laura wanted to identify with Cindy, she could. She could say to herself, "Yeah, I sure know about that!" But she didn't have to identify. She could give herself as much distance as she might want.

Then Santa said that freckles were as beautiful as the stars, Christmas tree lights, and the ocean at night. This wasn't me saying this to Laura; it was Santa saying it to Cindy. Laura didn't have to evaluate it.

Santa's letter also established Laura as a valued authority on freckles, a person to whom other people would turn for advice.

At our Christmas gathering, Laura greeted me with an enthusiastic hug, and handed me—with a big smile on her face—her reply to Santa. (I can't imagine how she knew to give the letter to me!)

⟨~⟩

Another situation involved a friend and his wife who are divorcing. The kids are very upset about it—especially nine-year-old Barbara. I wanted to say something supportive to her, but in an oblique way that she could relate to.

⟨~⟩

Santa's Workshop
The North Pole
Elfuary 139, 2003

Dear Barbara,

Elmer Zkllqmbap, the elf that watches over the children in Cedartown [a suburb of Atlanta] wrote me a letter yesterday. He said that your mother and daddy were not living together anymore, and that you were very sad about that.

I can understand that. Lots of my elves write and tell me about how unhappy it makes the children when their parents can't get along with each other. Sometimes the kids themselves write me.

Sandy, who lives just a couple miles from you, wrote me about the day her mother left. As she was walking out the door, Sandy grabbed her by the leg and begged her, "Mamma, please don't go! I'll behave, I promise! I'll be a good girl!"

Lots of kids think it is their fault that their parents can't get along with each other. But it is not your fault. Nobody in their right mind expects children to be perfect. Your parents weren't perfect when they were children, and neither are you. Lots of times, even though deep down Mother and Daddy may still love each other, they can't get along with each other and have to live apart. So if you think that is partly your fault, just remember that lots of other kids make that same mistake, even though it doesn't make any sense at all.

Michelle said she was afraid her mother and daddy didn't love her anymore. That doesn't make any sense either. Of course your mother and daddy love you and will protect you, and nothing is going to change that.

Sally lives in Atlanta. She wants to know if her mother and daddy will ever get back together again. I told her that nobody can know that. Some parents do get back together, and some don't. But whether they do or not, they will still love you and protect you.

Andrea, who lives on the other side of Cedartown, wrote me about how she couldn't sleep at night, and had nightmares, and had headaches. Lots of kids whose parents can't get along with each other have problems like this. I tell them to be patient. In just a little while, you will be sleeping better and your headaches will go away.

If you would like to write me, I would be glad to hear from you. Just give your letter to your daddy, and he will make sure I get it.

Love,
Santa

Other letters might address illness, death in the family, and so forth.

Letters from Santa can also be used as children's sermons. Issues that are common to most children can be phrased in terms of incidents among Santa's reindeer, elves, and helpers. The parable of the lost sheep, for instance, easily translates into a story about a young reindeer who doesn't make it to Santa's birthday party. Or Billy has dropped the Thanksgivving pie on the floor, and is afraid Santa will be angry at him.

A famous psychiatrist once said that psychotherapy should above all else be charming. So should children's sermons. A well-crafted letter from Santa has that potential.

To some, this chapter may seem inappropriate in a book on ceremonies, but certain features are similar. One of the important features of a ceremony is that it is led by someone who represents God (Santa), and also the broader community. It enlists other people, whether real or imaginary. Like the letters from Santa, a ceremony seeks first to establish rapport, and then put the difficulty in a different frame of reference.

Bibliography

Anderson, Herbert and Edward Foley (1997). *Mighty stories, dangerous rituals: Weaving together the human and the divine.* San Francisco: Jossey-Bass.

Bateson, Gregory ([1972] 2000). The cybernetics of "self": A theory of alcoholism. In Gregory Bateson, *Steps to an ecology of mind* (pp. 309-337). Chicago: University of Chicago Press.

Close, Henry T. (1999). *Metaphor in psychotherapy: Clinical applications of stories and allegories.* CA: Impact Publishers.

Close, Henry. (2004). *Becoming a forgiving person: A pastoral perspective.* Binghamton, NY: The Haworth Pastoral Press.

Gray, John (1992). *Men are from Mars, women are from Venus: A practical guide for improving communication and getting what you want in your relationship.* New York: HarperCollins.

Lamb, Jane M. (1989). *Bittersweet . . . hellogoodbye: A resource in planning farewell rituals when a baby dies.* St. Charles, MO: SHARE–Pregnancy and Infant Loss Support Inc.

Tannen, Deborah (1986). *That's not what I meant! How conversational style makes or breaks relationships.* New York: William Morrow.

Tannen, Deborah (1990). *You just don't understand: Women and men in conversation.* New York: William Morrow.

Toman, Walter (1993). *Family constellation: Its effects on personality and social behavior,* Fourth edition. New York: Springer.

Williamson, Marianne (1996). *A return to love: Reflections on the principles of "A Course in Miracles."* New York: HarperCollins.

doi:10.1300/5590_24

THE HAWORTH PASTORAL PRESS®
Pastoral Care, Ministry, and Spirituality
Richard Dayringer, ThD
Senior Editor

CEREMONIES FOR SPIRITUAL HEALING AND GROWTH by Henry Close

ASK ANYTHING: A PASTORAL THEOLOGY OF INQUIRY by Richard P. Olson

TRAINING GUIDE FOR VISITING THE SICK: MORE THAN A SOCIAL CALL by William G. Justice

BECOMING A FORGIVING PERSON: A PASTORAL PERSPECTIVE by Henry Close. "*Becoming A Forgiving Person* is a tender and compelling work that charts differing paths which lead to personal healing through the medium of forgiveness. Close's wisdom of psyche and soul come together in very practical ways through his myriad stories and illustrations." *Virginia Felder, MDiv, ThM, DMin, Licensed Professional Counselor, Licensed Marriage and Family Therapist, Private Practice, Dallas, TX*

TRANSFORMING SHAME: A PASTORAL RESPONSE by Jill L. McNish

A PASTORAL COUNSELOR'S MODEL FOR WELLNESS IN THE WORKPLACE: PSYCHERGONOMICS by Robert L. Menz. "This text is a must-read for chaplains and pastoral counselors wishing to understand and apply holistic health care to troubled employees, whether they be nurses, physicians, other health care workers, or workers in other industries. This book is filled with practical ideas and tools to help clergy care for the physical, mental, and spiritual needs of employees at the workplace." *Harold G. Koenig, MD, Associate Professor of Psychiatry, Duke University Medical Center; Author,* Chronic Pain: Biomedical and Spiritual Approaches

A THEOLOGY OF PASTORAL PSYCHOTHERAPY: GOD'S PLAY IN SACRED SPACES by Brian W. Grant. "Brian Grant's book is a compassionate and sophisticated synthesis of theology and psychoanalysis. His wise, warm grasp binds a community of healers with the personal qualities, responsibilities, and burdens of the pastoral psychotherapist." *David E. Scharff, MD, Co-Director, International Institute of Object Relations Therapy*

LIFE CYCLE: PSYCHOLOGICAL AND THEOLOGICAL PERCEPTIONS by Richard Dayringer

LOSSES IN LATER LIFE: A NEW WAY OF WALKING WITH GOD, SECOND EDITION by R. Scott Sullender. "Continues to be a timely and helpful book. There is an empathetic tone throughout, even though the book is a bold challenge to grieve for the sake of growth and maturity and faithfulness. . . . An important book." *Herbert Anderson, PhD, Professor of Pastoral Theology, Catholic Theological Union, Chicago, Illinois*

CARING FOR PEOPLE FROM BIRTH TO DEATH edited by James E. Hightower Jr. "An expertly detailed account of the hopes and hazards folks experience at each stage of their lives. Your empathy will be deepened and your care of people will be highly informed." *Wayne E. Oates, PhD, Professor of Psychiatry Emeritus, School of Medicine, University of Louisville, Kentucky*

HIDDEN ADDICTIONS: A PASTORAL RESPONSE TO THE ABUSE OF LEGAL DRUGS by Bridget Clare McKeever. "This text is a must-read for physicians, pastors, nurses, and counselors. It should be required reading in every seminary and Clinical Pastoral Education program." *Martin C. Helldorfer, DMin, Vice President, Mission, Leadership Development and Corporate Culture, Catholic Health Initiatives—Eastern Region, Pennsylvania*

THE EIGHT MASKS OF MEN: A PRACTICAL GUIDE IN SPIRITUAL GROWTH FOR MEN OF THE CHRISTIAN FAITH by Frederick G. Grosse. "Thoroughly grounded in traditional Christian spirituality and thoughtfully aware of the needs of men in our culture. . . . Close attention could make men's groups once again a vital spiritual force in the church." *Eric O. Springsted, PhD, Chaplain and Professor of Philosophy and Religion, Illinois College, Jacksonville, Illinois*

THE HEART OF PASTORAL COUNSELING: HEALING THROUGH RELATIONSHIP, REVISED EDITION by Richard Dayringer. "Richard Dayringer's revised edition of *The Heart of Pastoral Counseling* is a book for every person's pastor and a pastor's every person." *Glen W. Davidson, Professor, New Mexico Highlands University, Las Vegas, New Mexico*

WHEN LIFE MEETS DEATH: STORIES OF DEATH AND DYING, TRUTH AND COURAGE by Thomas W. Shane. "A kaleidoscope of compassionate, artfully tendered pastoral encounters that evoke in the reader a full range of emotions." *The Rev. Dr. James M. Harper, III, Corporate Director of Clinical Pastoral Education, Health Midwest; Director of Pastoral Care, Baptist Medical Center and Research Medical Center, Kansas City, Missouri*

A MEMOIR OF A PASTORAL COUNSELING PRACTICE by Robert L. Menz. "Challenges the reader's belief system. A humorous and abstract book that begs to be read again, and even again." *Richard Dayringer, ThD, Professor and Director, Program in Psychosocial Care, Department of Medical Humanities; Professor and Chief, Division of Behavioral Science, Department of Family and Community Medicine, Southern Illinois University School of Medicine*

Order a copy of this book with this form or online at:
http://www.haworthpress.com/store/product.asp?sku=5590

CEREMONIES FOR SPIRITUAL HEALING AND GROWTH

_____in hardbound at $29.95 (ISBN-13: 978-0-7890-2904-1; ISBN-10: 0-7890-2904-9)

_____in softbound at $19.95 (ISBN-13: 978-0-7890-2905-8; ISBN-10: 0-7890-2905-7)

Or order online and use special offer code HEC25 in the shopping cart.

COST OF BOOKS_____	☐ **BILL ME LATER:** (Bill-me option is good on US/Canada/Mexico orders only; not good to jobbers, wholesalers, or subscription agencies.)
POSTAGE & HANDLING_____ *(US: $4.00 for first book & $1.50 for each additional book)* *(Outside US: $5.00 for first book & $2.00 for each additional book)*	☐ Check here if billing address is different from shipping address and attach purchase order and billing address information. Signature_____
SUBTOTAL_____	☐ **PAYMENT ENCLOSED: $_____**
IN CANADA: ADD 7% GST_____	☐ **PLEASE CHARGE TO MY CREDIT CARD.**
STATE TAX_____ *(NJ, NY, OH, MN, CA, IL, IN, PA, & SD residents, add appropriate local sales tax)*	☐ Visa ☐ MasterCard ☐ AmEx ☐ Discover ☐ Diner's Club ☐ Eurocard ☐ JCB Account #_____
FINAL TOTAL_____ *(If paying in Canadian funds, convert using the current exchange rate, UNESCO coupons welcome)*	Exp. Date_____ Signature_____

Prices in US dollars and subject to change without notice.

NAME_____

INSTITUTION_____

ADDRESS_____

CITY_____

STATE/ZIP_____

COUNTRY_____ COUNTY (NY residents only)_____

TEL_____ FAX_____

E-MAIL_____

May we use your e-mail address for confirmations and other types of information? ☐ Yes ☐ No
We appreciate receiving your e-mail address and fax number. Haworth would like to e-mail or fax special discount offers to you, as a preferred customer. **We will never share, rent, or exchange your e-mail address or fax number.** We regard such actions as an invasion of your privacy.

Order From Your Local Bookstore or Directly From
The Haworth Press, Inc.
10 Alice Street, Binghamton, New York 13904-1580 • USA
TELEPHONE: 1-800-HAWORTH (1-800-429-6784) / Outside US/Canada: (607) 722-5857
FAX: 1-800-895-0582 / Outside US/Canada: (607) 771-0012
E-mail to: orders@haworthpress.com

For orders outside US and Canada, you may wish to order through your local
sales representative, distributor, or bookseller.
For information, see http://haworthpress.com/distributors

(Discounts are available for individual orders in US and Canada only, not booksellers/distributors.)

PLEASE PHOTOCOPY THIS FORM FOR YOUR PERSONAL USE.
http://www.HaworthPress.com   BOF06